PLACE IN RETURN BOX to remove this checkout from your r̶
TO AVOID FINES return on or before d̶

DATE DU

The Butler Commentaries on Soviet Law

Fundamental Principles of Legislation on Investment Activity in the USSR and Republics

The Butler
Commentaries on Soviet Law
General Editor: Professor W. E. Butler

FUNDAMENTAL PRINCIPLES OF LEGISLATION ON INVESTMENT ACTIVITY IN THE USSR AND REPUBLICS

Commentary by

M. I. Braginskii, W. E. Butler, A. A. Rubanov

Translated by

W. E. Butler

INTERLIST

London & Moscow

1991

Fundamental Principles of Legislation on Investment Activity in the USSR and Republics

(The Butler Commentaries)

I.Butler,W.E. II.Braginskii,M.I. III.Rubanov,A.A.

IV. Series 343.47052

ISBN 1-873461-04-6

ISSN 0963-3340

First published in 1991 by INTERLIST
a division of Intershelf Ltd.
6 Cavendish Square, London, W1 9HA

Printed in Great Britain

CONTENTS

Section I: General Provisions

Section II: Effectuation of Investment Activity

Section III: State Regulation of Investment Activity

Table of Contents

Section IV: Guarantees of Rights and Protection of Investments

ANNEXES

ABBREVIATIONS

FPCivL	Fundamental Principles of Civil Legislation of the USSR and Union Republics (1961) *or* Fundamental Principles of Civil Legislation of the USSR and Republics (1991)
FPCivProc	Fundamental Principles of Legislation of the USSR and Union Republics on Civil Procedure (1961)
FPCrimL	Fundamental Principles of Criminal Legislation of the USSR and Union Republics (1958) or (1991)
FPCrimP	Fundamental Principles of Legislation on Criminal Procedure of the USSR and Union Republics (1958)
FPForest	Fundamental Principles of the USSR and Union Republics on Forestry Legislation (1977)
FPForInv	Fundamental Principles of Legislation on Foreign Investments in the USSR (1991)
FPInvA	Fundamental Principles of Legislation on Investment Activity in the USSR
FPLand	Fundamental Principles of Land Legislation of the USSR and Union Republics
FPLease	Fundamental Principles of Legislation of the USSR on the Lease
RSFSR	Russian Soviet Federated Socialist Republic

SP SSSR	*Sobranie postanovlenii pravitel'stva SSSR*
USSR	Union of Soviet Socialist Republics
Vedomosti SND RSFSR	*Vedomosti s"ezda narodnykh deputatov i verkhovnogo soveta RSFSR*
Vedomosti SND SSSR	*Vedomosti s"ezda narodnykh deputatov i verkhovnogo soveta SSSR*
Vedomosti SSSR	*Vedomosti verkhovnogo soveta SSSR*

INTRODUCTION

This volume continues the series of Commentaries on individual all-union and republic legislative acts of key importance to the foreign business, commercial, legal, financial, and academic communities.

The Commentary is a traditional form of gloss widely employed in the prerevolutionary Russian and Soviet legal traditions to guide and assist judges, arbitrators, jurisconsults, advocates, and other legal professionals in interpreting and applying a particular Law, Code, or other enactment. Here, uniquely, the Commentary is the joint product of Western and Russian specialists with vast experience in East-West legal affairs, including the draughting of Soviet legislation at the all-union, republic, and local levels. The authors collectively comprise a Working Group appointed to assist the Commission for Economic Reform of the USSR Council of Ministers in evaluating and preparing draft Union legislation from the standpoint of international standards and foreign practice.

The Commentary also follows a standard format: an English translation of the full text of the Fundamental Principles of Legislation on Investment Activity in the USSR with an article-by-article, point-by-point explication of the background and provisions of the Law. Appended are translations of three further enactments: the Decree of the USSR Supreme Soviet on the procedure for introducing the Fundamental Principles into effect; the Edict of the President of the USSR dated 26 October 1990 on foreign investments in the USSR; and the Fundamental Principles of Legislation on Foreign Investments in the USSR adopted on 5 July 1991.

For a general introduction to the Soviet legal system, the reader is referred to W. E. Butler, *Soviet Law* (2d ed., London: Butterworths, 1988).

FUNDAMENTAL PRINCIPLES OF LEGISLATION ON INVESTMENT ACTIVITY IN THE USSR

[Adopted by the USSR Supreme Soviet, 10 December 1990. *Vedomosti SND SSSR* (1990) no. 51, item 1109]

1

Investment Activity

[PREAMBLE]

The present Fundamental Principles determine the general legal, economic, and social conditions of investment activity on the territory of the USSR. They are directed towards ensuring the equal protection of the rights, interests, and property of subjects of investment activity irrespective of the forms of ownership and the effective functioning of the national economy of the USSR under conditions of the market economy.

1. The existence of a preamble is comparatively rare for Soviet legislation of the perestroika era. Before 1985 major all-union laws had preambles as a rule which were rather extensive and contained a rather general discourse with propagandistic overtones.

The FPInvA here follows the old pattern but briefly and without being propagandistic. The preamble is used to set out the aims and objectives of the FPInvA. While this is to be preferred over the general discourse, the FPInvA all the same does not undertake the "self-analysis" in a fully objective manner.

2. The preamble declares that the FPInvA is directed towards serving the market economy. This assertion must be accepted with a serious reservation. In fact, the principal provisions of the FPInvA are directed towards serving the administrative-command system. To be sure there are norms in the FPInvA having a market orientation. But they have a secondary place and taken in

aggregate do not create the legal infrastructure of the market. At best they merely note certain of its features.

It is no accident that the FPInvA is contradictory in this respect. When the FPInvA was adopted the Soviet Union was at an historic turning point. The issue was whether there should be an economy based on directive planning or one based on the market. The choice was difficult for many reasons, amongst them ideological considerations. For decades the view was held in official ideology that the economy of the Soviet Union should be of a planned character and that a market economy would lead to production anarchy and crises. The entire policy was built pursuant to this notion: the leadership of the Soviet Union not only rejected the market, but implemented measures directed towards displacing commodity production in general.

In the course of perestroika since 1985 it was first declared that socio-economic development would accelerate, and when this did not happen, radical economic reform was undertaken. But it remained unclear as to the direction the reform would pursue. The view finally emerged that development should proceed towards creating an economy based on the market. This idea met serious resistance, but the economic position of the Soviet Union continued to worsen. On 13 July 1990 the USSR Supreme Soviet adopted a decree which provided: "to consider the transition to market relations the principal content of the radical economic reform."

Almost at once, however, the notion of the so-called third path was put forward. There were various views as to what this meant. Some believed that a market should be created in the Soviet Union that would have special qualities allowing it to be regarded as a socialist market; others suggested that it must be a "planned market." The

[Preamble]

Basic Orientations for the Stabilisation of the National Economy and Transition to a Market Economy," approved by the USSR Supreme Soviet on 19 October 1990,[1] spoke of the creation of a "socially-orientated market economy." When the FPInvA was enacted, the notion of the "third path" had been more clearly outlined. A number of officials began to speak in late 1990 about the use of the administrative-command system as a means for ensuring the movement of the economy towards a market one.

The FPInvA was adopted when that idea began to acted upon and was thus the first all-union law to be structured in accordance with the "third path." The principal provisions of the FPInvA preserve and perfect the administrative-command system in the domain of investing and secondarily create certain possibilities for movement towards the market economy.

The approach of the FPInvA towards the State as a participant of investment activity is worthy of attention in this connection. Under the administrative-command system the State is the principal figure in the sphere of investment: investment is primarily from budget sources and not repayable and is effectuated through directive planning, whereas in market-economy countries the State plays a secondary role in investment.

In the FPInvA the State is at the centre, which is consistent with its role in an administrative-command system. Virtually every Article of the FPInvA speaks about the State in one connection or another. Moreover, all of Section III of the FPInvA is given over to the State; other subjects of the FPInvA are not given so much attention.

---

[1]   *Vedomosti SND SSSR* (1990) no. 44, item 906.

5

There are also rules in the FPInvA where the State seemingly moves back to planning tasks. Usually this occurs where some sort of list is given, and the State is mentioned last. For example, when enumerating the subjects of investment activity, the State is placed last and citizens, first. This positioning does not correspond to their real role (see Commentary to Article 4[1]) but it is consistent with that role which the State plays in market economy countries on the capital market. Against a general background such norms are merely a means of demonstrating the "market intentions" of the legislator.

Having secured for the State a dominant role in the domain of investment, the FPInvA departed from the Basic Orientations for the Stabilisation of the National Economy and Transition to a Market Economy of 19 October 1990. The latter provided for the "renunciation by the State of direct participation in economic activity (except for individual special domains)." It was decided that such a renunciation must be made above all in the domain of investment. They contemplated suspending the fulfilment of investment programmes which do not meet national economic requirements, closing a significant portion of construction sites of production designation, prohibiting the installation of objects not secured by construction capacities, and the like. Notwithstanding this, the FPInvA has devoted a significant portion of its provisions to the direct administration of State investments (Articles 12-18).

The dual nature of the FPInvA makes it impossible to predict its future. If the movement of the Soviet Union towards an economy based on the market is not sustained, the FPInvA will remain one of those laws typical of the administrative-command system and the norms of a market orientation will be an historical curiosity. But if the movement towards the market continues, the FPInvA provisions which improve the administrative-command system will become a survival of the past and the norms of a market character will provide material for further legislation creating the market infrastructure.

3. The preamble affirms that the FPInvA determines not only the legal, but also the economic and even the social conditions of investment activity. Here the FPInvA greatly exaggerates its role and significance. Its rules are decisive for the legal aspect of investment activity. The economic and, even more, the social conditions are determined by circumstances lying far outside the law. The FPInvA can exert merely an indirect and secondary influence on them.

4. The preamble specifies that a purpose of the FPInvA is to ensure the effectiveness of the functioning of the national economy of the USSR. This also requires commentary.

It is helpful that the FPInvA itself indicates what purpose it pursues. This enables the means selected by it and the character of its basic provisions to be evaluated more precisely. The FPInvA sets out a tempting but regrettably unrealistic purpose. The FPInvA was adopted on 10 December 1990, that is, when the economy of the Soviet Union had begun to slip into a serious and deepening economic crisis. To imagine then how the effectiveness of the national economy might be secured was unrealistic. It would have been more proper rather to be concerned with stabilising it and working out measures in the domain of legal regulation of investment activity that would lead to this aim being achieved.

In addition, the purpose declared by the FPInvA presupposes that the FPInvA itself must in all respects be a legally perfected law. Only a carefully thought-out and crafted enactment can ensure that the national economy functions efficiently. But candour is required here, and it must be said that the FPInvA does not meet the requisite standard in all respects.

It contains norms which have been formulated unsatisfactorily, including with respect to issues of enormous importance for the expansion of investment activities. There are gaps with regard to several questions, such that the silence of the FPInvA makes it possible to restrain the development of investments. Many articles of the FPInvA are unjustifiably devoted to sundry definitions and all too often norms are purely declaratory. Many articles do not resolve issues, but rather refer to other legislative acts. A major shortcoming of the FPInvA is the numerous repetitions. And there are internal inconsistencies in the FPInvA.

As a whole, the FPInvA juridically speaking is well below the standard of the other laws adopted since 1985. Inevitably there will be many significant practical difficulties in implementing it.

5. The Preamble of the FPInvA proclaims as one of its purposes the ensuring of the equal protection of subjects of investment activity irrespective of the forms of ownership.

Soviet law is structured on the principle that some things are recognised by law as a form of ownership, but not others. The concept of "form of ownership" has no precisely established content. There exists merely a certain general understanding that recognising certain things as a form of ownership is linked with the fact that those things play an especially significant socio-economic role. The list of forms of ownership is contained in the 1990 USSR Law on Ownership: "Ownership in the USSR shall take the form of the ownership of Soviet citizens and collective and State ownership."[2] That Law further mentions mixed forms of ownership (Article 4[2]) and provides that "other forms of ownership not provided for by the present Law may be established by legislative acts of the union and autonomous republics" (Article 4[3]). However, although the Law provides that the ownership of foreign States, international organisations, and foreign juridical persons and citizens "may exist" in the USSR, such ownership is not recognised to be a form of ownership.

6. The Preamble indicates that the FPInvA determines the legal conditions for investment activity "on the territory of the USSR." The USSR Constitution establishes that the territory of the USSR is integral and incorporates the territories of the union republics.[3] The FPInvA consequently regulates investment activity throughout the Soviet Union.

The reference to the territory of the USSR relates to internal aspects of the operation of the FPInvA. The provision should not be understood to be a rule establishing the territorial character of the FPInvA. In Soviet law the international aspects of the operation of laws fall into the domain of private international law. The

[2]   Article 4(1). *Vedomosti SSSR* (1990) no. 11, item 164; transl. in M. I. Braginskii, W. E. Butler, and A. A. Rubanov (commentary), *The Law on Ownership in the USSR* (1991) p. 51.

[3]   Article 75, USSR Constitution. Translated in W. E. Butler (ed.) *Basic Documents on the Soviet Legal System* (2d ed., 1991) p. 17

FPInvA contains no provisions obstructing the application of its provisions by foreign courts when conflicts rules refer to Soviet law.

7. The enactment begins with the words: Fundamental Principles. This is the first law in the Soviet Union to refer in its title not to the Fundamental Principles of Legislation of the USSR and Union Republics, but simply to Fundamental Principles of Legislation. Previously all laws using the term "Fundamental Principles" always indicated that one was speaking of Fundamental Principles emanating from the USSR and for legislation adopted by the union republics. This is a departure from the USSR Constitution, which provides that "the establishment of fundamental principles of legislation of the USSR and union republics" is subject to the jurisdiction of the USSR.[4]

This formulation of the title of the FPInvA was a reaction to the crisis which existed at the time it was adopted in relations between the Union and the union republics. Throughout 1990 all the union republics and many autonomous republics adopted Declarations on their sovereignty. Some, notably the largest -- the Russian Federation and the Ukraine -- issued laws according to which republic laws enjoy supreme legal force in comparison with laws of the USSR.

Under these circumstances the all-union legislator preferred not to indicate in the title of the FPInvA that he was creating fundamental principles for union republic legislation. But that was cosmetic. In substance the FPInvA proceeds from the fact that it must serve as the

---

[4]   Article 73(4) USSR Constitution. Transl. in W. E. Butler (ed.), *Basic Documents on the Soviet Legal System* (2d ed., 1991) pp. 16-17.

[Preamble]

basis for union republic legislation. This is expressly mentioned in Article 5(1) below, where it stipulates that legislative acts of the union and autonomous republics must conform to the FPInvA (see Commentary to Article 5)

Investment Activity

Section I: General Provisions

Investment Activity

Article 1: Investments

All types of property and intellectual valuables contributed to objects of entrepreneurial and other types of activity, as a result of which profit (or revenue) is formed or a social effect is achieved, shall be investments.

Such valuables may be:

monetary assets, special purpose bank deposits, shares, stocks, and other securities

movable and immovable property (buildings, installations, equipment, and other material valuables)

property rights arising from copyright, "know-how" experience, and other intellectual valuables

rights of the use of land and other natural resources, as well as other property rights

other valuables.

Investments in the regeneration of basic funds may be effectuated in the form of capital investments.

1.   This Section of the FPInvA, bearing the heading "General Provisions" endeavours to formulate those provisions which would be theoretically well-founded. This is a desirable and positive endeavour. But this purpose is not achieved and the effort is merely an attempt to achieve doctrinal respectability.

To some extent this is explainable. The theoretical studies which underlie other major all-union legislative acts have been underway for many years. The legislator merely relied upon their conclusions. The FPInvA had no such possibility since Soviet legal doctrine had never conducted theoretical research into the legal regulation of relations connected with investing.

The legislator attempted to autonomously resolve certain basic problems. It is no surprise that in most cases he did not succeed: the FPInvA is concerned with its problems, and the legal scholar, with his.

We note two basic manifestations of the FPInvA endeavour to achieve doctrinal respectability. When structuring the Section on "General Provisions," the scheme for ordering the Articles was drawn from elementary civil law textbooks. The textbooks, as a rule, commence by considering what relations are regulated by civil law, and then pass on to the objects of those relations, and then consider questions relating to the subjects of those relations. The sequence of Articles in the FPInvA is analogous: it commences with Articles on investments (Article 1) and investment activity (Article 2) then passes on to the Article on the objects of investment activity (Article 3) and then to the subjects of investment activity (Article 4).

Another manifestation of the same aspiration is that the FPInvA contains many provisions defining various concepts: investments, objects of entrepreneurial activity, investment activity, investors, participants of investment activity, and others.

The FPInvA apparently intends to stimulate the further development of legislation and legal science by beginning to isolate norms affecting relations connected with investing; that is, to those processes which ultimately would lead to the creation of an autonomous branch of law: "investment law."

If the draughtsman truly had this in view, then the purpose was not achieved. Soviet law is divided into branches on the basis of indicia which are objectively inherent in relations regulated by the respective branch of law. The relations connected with investments are heterogeneous. To combine them in a single category is impossible. They are regulated by various branches of law. Therefore there exists no theoretical basis for the existence of "investment law" as an individual branch of law.

The fact that there are too many definitions included in the FPInvA does not help the formation of a new branch of investment law either. Experience shows that definitions incorporated in a law are successful only when they have been thoroughly worked out in doctrine, and even then they lead to controversy. Many definitions in the FPInvA show every sign of having been improvised by the legislator.

The use of economic categories and concepts is a serious defect in many provisions of the FPInvA. The aim of every law is the legal regulation of relations. Concepts borrowed from works of economists usually are not helpful, although they can help shed light on the general meaning of a law. But precise legal regulation can not be based on them.

This "economic accent" is not peculiar only to the FPInvA. It is to be found in a number of other laws adopted in the Soviet Union during perestroika, reflecting the fact that economists have played an active role in legislation. Many in the Soviet Union await their answer of how to reform the economy. In the FPInvA their influence is more noticeable than in other legislative enactments.

2. The definition of investments in paragraph one of this Article is an economic definition and is capable of playing a positive role in Soviet legislation if the economy moves towards the market economy.

In other legal systems such a definition might seem superfluous. However, in Soviet law its appearance merits attention. In this rule the FPInvA describes and consequently juridically sanctions the turnover of capital; that is, the movement of valuables pursuant to which it is deposited for activity as a result of which a new, larger valuable will be created -- profit. This indeed is an elementary outline of capital turnover.

In order to properly evaluate the socio-political significance of the fact that a law recognises there is capital turnover in the Soviet Union and consequently that capital itself exists, one must recall that here the FPInvA has departed from one of the principal ideological views regarding the Soviet economy which dominated economic, political, and legal life for decades.

The so-called political economy of socialism enjoys enormous influence in the Soviet Union. Outwardly this is a doctrine claiming to exhaustively explain the economic system of the Soviet Union. It was developed by Soviet economists, especially since the mid-1930s. It was taught in Soviet institutions of higher education as an instructional discipline. Countless books, articles, and pamphlets have been written about the political economy of socialism. The proponents of this doctrine have constantly adapted this theory to the changing utterances of Soviet political leaders on economic issues, and indeed it was formed as a sort of supplement to the views formulated by the founders of Marxist doctrine. The theory of the latter was called the "political economy of capitalism."

The principal task of the "political economy of socialism" was to substantiate the assertion that the Soviet economy would always develop only upwards. The founders of Marxism had concluded that the Western economy contemporary to them was undergoing crises and ultimately would perish. The proponents of the "political economy of socialism" built their theoretical notions on the principle of juxtaposing those views which on analogous issues had been uttered by the founders of Marxist doctrine. For example, if it was asserted that a certain phenomenon in the economy of the West inevitably leads to crises, then within the framework of the "political economy of socialism" it would be commonly asserted that such phenomena do not exist in the Soviet economy.

The view with respect to capital in particular was so formulated. The founders of Marxist doctrine believed that capital is not the sum of accumulated wealth but rather a special relation between people. In their view the means of production and money itself were not capital. They were transformed into capital only when hired labour appeared on the scene. In such instances, asserted the founders of this doctrine, there occurs the exploitation of hired workers, which causes class struggle.

The orthodox proponents of the "political economy of socialism" categorically deny that exploitation occurs under the economic system existing in the Soviet Union. This is substantiated by the assertion that hired labour is completely absent. In substance this is nothing more than an ideological position. In reality millions of people work in State enterprises on the basis of contracts and receive wages for their labour. In the "political economy of socialism" the thesis that there is no hired labour underlies a number of other ideological postulates. One is that a category such as capital can not exist in the USSR; that is, capital in the sense put forward by the founders of Marxist doctrine. But capital in general has become an ideological taboo. The proponents of such an ideology would allow means of production and money to exist in the USSR, but reject the notion that they act as capital since hired labour does not exist.

The optimistic statements of the proponents of the "political economy of socialism" that the Soviet Union has unlimited opportunities for economic development have been criticised under glasnost. The assertion is disputed that exploitation and hired labour do not exist. However, there remains some restraint when addressing the issue of capital. Some critics maintain that the Soviet economy is a form of State capitalism. But they are careful and refrain from acknowledging the existence of capital as such.

The step taken by the FPInvA against this background is rather radical. The FPInvA expressly has acknowledged that a process occurs in the Soviet Union characteristic of capital turnover: the investment of cash and material valuables in activity which will entail the appearance of profit.

To be sure, in matters of terminology the FPInvA has genuflected to the traditions of the "political economy of socialism." The term "capital" is not used, as in preceding decades it has taken on a negative ideological colouration; instead the neutral terms "investments" and "valuables" are used.

3. Paragraph one of this Article schematically describes the capital market by juxtaposing two aspects: investments and the objects of entrepreneurial activity.

One might take the view that a legislative enactment should not sketch in this way. However, Soviet law is in a special situation. For more than seven decades there has been no capital market in the Soviet Union. Even the general notion of what a capital market is has been erased from the social consciousness. Hence this provision of the FPInvA may play a positive role.

Both aspects are described not from the legal, but from the economic point of view. The FPInvA speaks not about subjects operating in the market, but about economic categories which are present there.

The first of these are defined in the FPInvA as "valuables." In and of itself this is a broad expression. Nonetheless, the FPInvA adds that "all types" of valuables are permitted in the market and specially emphasises that reference is being made not only to property, but also to intellectual valuables.

In this provision the FPInvA confines itself to an economic characterisation, but in a number of other Articles the legal aspects are regulated in detail as regards the investment market (see Commentary to Article 2[2]).

The other aspect of the market has been defined as the objects of entrepreneurial activity. It follows from the FPInvA that activity is "entrepreneurial" when as a consequence thereof profit or revenue is created. The FPInvA also places alongside objects of other types of activity, as a consequence whereof a social effect is created.

Although in this case the FPInvA describes the recipients of investments in terms which at first glance seem very broad, this description actually suffers from a serious defect. The FPInvA speaks only of presently existing objects of entrepreneurial and other activity. But investment in objects to be newly created plays a major role in the investment market. When investment commences, those objects do not exist. Investment is essential so that they might be created. Otherwise a market economy could not exist.

The silence of the FPInvA on such investment is astonishing. There is no doubt that private entrepreneurial activity must be permitted. The discussion is merely over the scale of such activity. The objects of such activity at the moment the FPInvA was adopted would be new objects. To leave them outside the investment market is to obstruct the development of private entrepreneurial activity.

A typical feature of the FPInvA is the absence of provisions characterising juridically the recipients of investments. Whereas the FPInvA says little about the possessors of investments, nothing whatever is said about the potential recipients. The FPInvA confines itself to an economic characterisation of them as the objects of entrepreneurial or other activity. The FPInvA even does not mention them in the Article specially devoted to the participants of investment activity (see Commentary to Article 4[3]).

4. The mutual relations of investments and objects of entrepreneurial activity are characterised by the FPInvA as an"investment." The FPInvA contains no norms which enable one to ascertain what an investment is. One may merely conclude that the investment of valuables, as distinct from alienating them, gives rise to a link between the contributor and the object of entrepreneurial activity.

This link might be extremely various, both economically and legally. One type of link arises under the administrative-command system with budget investment without repayment; the State contributes assets to State objects by way of directive planning. Another type of link occurs in the investment market, where a contract is the basis of the link.

A contract underlies the most diverse of relations. For example, an "investment" based on a loan contract concluded by a bank with an enterprise differs from an "investment" through the purchase of stocks of a joint-stock society. Likewise, the "investment" of a building or installation in the charter fund of a joint enterprise formed by a Soviet juridical person and a Western firm is very different from a publishing contract concluded by the author of a work of literature with a publishing house, and the like.

5.   Article 1, paragraph two, of the FPInvA contains a list of individual types of valuables which figure in the investment market. This is a clarification of the general rule that all types of valuables are permitted in the market. It is useful and perhaps even essential. In the time that has elapsed since 1917 the social consciousness has forgotten what the capital market is.

The list is not exhaustive. It includes four groups of valuables which in practice most often figure in the investment market.

The first group constitutes cash assets, special-purpose bank deposits, shares, as well as stocks and other securities.

Cash assets are accorded first mention since market investments are principally in monetary form. The concepts of cash assets encompasses any currency, both Soviet and foreign. As regards their correlation, one should note that according to the USSR Law "On the State Bank of the USSR" of 11 December 1990, the State Bank of the USSR regulates the exchange rate of the ruble with respect to the monetary units of foreign States by establishing the official exchange rate quotations and performing operations regarding the sale and purchase of foreign currency for rubles on the free currency market.[5]

The concept of special-purpose bank deposits has not arisen in other all-union laws. The reference is not to deposits in a bank but, on the contrary, to deposits of a bank in objects of entrepreneurial activity. Juridically this is not a deposit, but a contract of loan under which the bank acts as the lender. A bank loan in Soviet law traditionally has a special-purpose character, in connection with which the bank is given the right to control the use of the amounts received in the bank.

A share is a portion of the assets contributed to the object of entrepreneurial activity belonging to several possessors. Prevailing legislation speaks of shares in housing-construction and dacha-construction cooperatives.

Among the valuables of the first group, stocks and other securities are of great importance. The concept of securities and stocks is defined by the Statute on Securities, confirmed by the USSR Council of Ministers on 19 June 1990.[6] Securities are monetary documents certifying the right of possession or relations of loan

5   Article 18. *Vedomosti SND SSSR* (1990) no. 52, item 1154

6   *SP SSSR* (1990) no. 15, item 82; transl. in W. E. Butler (ed.), *Basic Documents on the Soviet Legal System* (2d ed., 1991) pp. 345-353

determining the relations between the person who issued those documents and the possessors thereof and providing, as a rule, for the payment of revenue in the form of dividends or interest, as well as the possibility of the transfer of monetary or other rights arising from such documents to other persons (Article 1). Among such securities are bonds, treasury obligations of the State, savings certificates, bills of exchange, and stocks.

The Statute on Securities defines a stock as a security issued by joint-stock societies, enterprises, organisations, commercial banks, cooperative, and other enterprises and organisations based on collective ownership or on full economic jurisdiction of State ownership without an established period of circulation which certifies the contribution of assets for the purposes of their development (membership in a joint-stock society or participation in its management) and giving the right to its possessor to receive part of the profit of the enterprise in the form of a dividend (Article 3). Joint-stock societies in the USSR have just begun to appear. By early 1991 several thousand joint-stock societies had been registered.[7]

The Statute on Securities distinguishes among three categories of stocks. The first category is the stocks of the labour collective, which are distributed only among the workers of its enterprise and are not subject to alienation to citizens who are not members of that labour collective. The Moscow Ventilator Plant was one of the first joint-stock enterprises of this type in the domain of producing means of production. All the property of the plant (valued at 6.5 million rubles) was divided into stocks with a par value of 200 rubles and offered to workers of the plant for purchase. Each was required to pay only 25%

---

[7]   See *Argumenty i fakty*, no. 7 (1991) p. 5, which indicates 1,200 were registered at the end of 1990.

down on their purchase. The remaining three-quarters was paid by a credit granted to the plant, which would be repaid from future dividends. Some 300 of the 500 workers at the plant became stockholders.[8]

The second category is the stocks of enterprises. They are distributed among other enterprises and organisations, voluntary societies, banks, and cooperatives. The third category is the stocks of joint-stock societies distributed by means of open subscription or by way of distribution of all stocks among the founders.

Valuables in the form of things are relegated to the second group. It is remarkable that the FPInvA introduced the division of things into movables and immovables. Previously Soviet law had rejected this for reasons of principle. The 1922 RSFSR Civil Code had provided: "with the abolition of private ownership of land, the division of property into movable and immovable has been eliminated" (Note to Article 12). The FPInvA has introduced this division without mentioning a change of position with regard to private ownership of land.

In the third group first mentioned are the property rights arising from copyright. The principal of these are the right of the author to publication, reproduction, and dissemination of his work. Another is the important right to give consent to the translation of a work into another language for the purposes of publication.

The property rights arising from the law of inventions is not included in the list, although the right to the exclusive use of an invention may become in the future market one of the principal investments in entrepreneurial activity. The silence of the FPInvA is not without reason. For decades the prevailing law of inventions has been based on anti-market principles, proceeding from the general idea that inventions should enter into production through centrally compiled plans. The inventions law correspondingly was directed towards concentrating in the hands of the State the right to use the principal mass of inventions created in the Soviet Union. The State determined by way of planning which of its enterprises should use specific inventions.

Until recently, the author's certificate has been the dominant form of protecting the right to an invention. An inventor, having obtained such a certificate, acquires the right to receive remuneration and transfers to the State the exclusive right to use of the invention. However, the 1991 FPCivL and the 1991 USSR Law on Inventions in the USSR did away with the author's certificate and protects the right to an invention only through the issuance of a patent, the right to the exclusive use of an invention belonging to the patentholder.[9] This reform was a step in the direction of the market economy. However, when the FPInvA was enacted, this step had not been taken.

In the fourth group are the right to use land and other natural resources.

The concept of "other natural resources" is encountered in other legislation. The 1990 USSR Law on Ownership mentions "land and its minerals, waters, and flora and fauna."[10] The FPInvA recognises the right of use of those objects to be investments and thereby they may be contributed to the market.

---

[9]   For the 1991 FPCivL, see W. E. Butler (ed.), *The USSR Fundamental Principles of Civil Legislation* (1991). The 1991 Law on Inventions in the USSR was adopted on the same date, 31 May 1991, but entered into force six months earlier, on 1 July 1991. See *Izvestiia*, 14 June 1991, pp. 4-5.

[10]   Article 20. See M. I. Braginskii, W. E. Butler, and A. A. Rubanov (commentary), *The Law on Ownership in the USSR* (1991), p. 203.

Under these circumstances the FPInvA merely mentions the right to use land and not the right of ownership in land in connection with valuables.

Finally, the FPInvA includes all other types of property rights in this group, without any exceptions or limitations. By property rights are contemplated not only rights, the object of which is a thing, but also those rights which can be expressed in monetary terms.

6. The rule contained in Article 1, paragraph three, throws additional light on the potential recipient of investments. The law explains that when investments are made in an object of entrepreneurial activity, they may be directed towards the regeneration of basic funds. In such instances they may acquire a respective form; namely, the form of capital investments.

This gloss may prove to be useful as the Soviet Union moves towards the market economy. It should be borne in mind that during the long decades of the predominance of the administrative-command system the basic funds of an enterprise were regarded as something sacred. Their regeneration occurred on the basis of various kinds of plans and was financed basically from State sources, mostly centrally appropriated assets.

The question of land deserves special attention. It is vital on both the general plane and as regards entrepreneurial activity. The latter is impossible without the requisite territorial base. The legal regime of land is among the major political and economic issues of perestroika confronting the Soviet Union. The 1990 USSR Law on Ownership contains two different provisions regarding land. One provides that land is the inalienable weal of the peoples residing on a particular territory (Article 20), whereas another establishes that land may be in ownership (Article 3[1]). The RSFSR and some other union republics have enacted legislation permitting land plots to be in private ownership.[11]   The rise of the investment market has led to pluralism in sources for financing enterprises. The provision here considered stresses that the regeneration of basic funds also will occur under conditions of such pluralism and that all assets received for this purpose from various sources will have the form of capital investments.

The FPInvA does not mention here the circulating funds of an enterprise. But elsewhere the FPInvA expressly provides for investing also in circulating funds (see Commentary to Article 3).

---

[11]   See Articles 2 and 7, RSFSR Land Code, adopted 25 April 1991. *Rossiiskaia gazeta*, 23 May 1991, pp. 3-7. While private ownership of land is permitted under this Code, such ownership is related to the purposes for which the land is to be used. Onerous conditions limiting the marketability of land may be introduced by the agency disposing of the land to citizens.

Investment Activity

Article 2: Investment Activity

1. By investment activity is understood the aggregate of practical activities of citizens, juridical persons, and States relating to the realisation of investment activity.

2.   Investment activity shall be effectuated on the basis of:

investing effectuated by citizens, non-State enterprises, economic associations, societies, and partnerships, as well as by social and religious organisations, and other juridical persons based on collective ownership;

State investing effectuated by agencies of power and administration of the USSR, union and autonomous republics, autonomous national areas and regions, other administrative-territorial formations at the expense of assets of budgets, extrabudgetary funds, and borrowed assets, as well as by State enterprises and institutions from their own and from borrowed assets;

foreign investing effectuated by foreign citizens, juridical persons, and States;

joint investing effectuated by Soviet and foreign citizens and juridical persons and States.

1.   This definition appears in the FPInvA in an effort to establish its doctrinal respectability. The 1991 FPCivL

establishes that such relations are regulated by civil legislation. The FPInvA attempts to follow the same path. This is tempting since the branches of Soviet law traditionally are structured to correspond to the relations which are regulated by legal norms. To set out in legislation which relations are regulated by the norms of investment legislation would be to make a serious step forward in the direction of creating "investment law."

In Article 5 below, the FPInvA used the concept of "relations connected with the effectuation of investment activity." However, they are not able to give a definition of them since this already has been done in the civil law. Instead the FPInvA defines investment activity.

However, the FPInvA thereby has demonstrated the impossibility of separating out a special branch of law which would rest on a special category of relations and not on a special type of activity.

2. The concept of investment activity was not discussed in Soviet doctrinal writings before the adoption of the FPInvA. The definition given is an extemporaneous one of the legislator.

The concept is used in many norms of the FPInvA. It even is used in the title of the FPInvA. Further, it underlies a number of other concepts extensively utilised in the FPInvA: the notion of objects of investment activity (Article 3); of subjects of investment activity (Article 4); of participants of investment activity (Article 4[3]); of the effectuation of investment activity (Article 6); of State regulation of investment activity (Article 10); of State regulation of the conditions of investment activity (Article 11); and others.

The definition of investment activity contained in this Article is consequently key to the entire FPInvA. Unfortunately, the definition is seriously deficient. The provision that "by investment activity is understood the aggregate ... of activities ... relating to the realisation ..." of investments contains an error of logic: one unknown is defined through another unknown. The FPInvA contains no definition of the realisation of investments. Further, Article 2(1) is the only place in the FPInvA where the "realisation" of investments is mentioned.

The FPInvA, however, contains another definition: "all types of property and intellectual valuables ... shall be investments" (Article 1). Therefore the "realisation" of investments is the realisation of those valuables. Under this approach the concept of investment activity can encompass everything that it is advantageous to include.

3.   The definition contained in Article 2(1) casts light on the basic positions and purposes of the FPInvA.

There are contradictions between the definition and the provisions in Article 2(2). The latter provisions refer to State investing effectuated by the USSR or the union or autonomous republics. Moreover, it speaks of the possibility of "foreign investing effectuated by foreign ... States." This last provision is linked with the development of market relations (see Commentary to Article 4[1]).

It should be noted that when the FPInvA formulates the definition of investment activity, it speaks of citizens and juridical persons in the plural, but of the State only in the singular. The FPInvA is thus orientated towards the situation which traditionally existed under the administrative-command system before 1985. One truly did have in view then investing by a single State, since the USSR was formally a federation but in substance a unitary State, the latter circumstance especially reflected in the fact that the budgets of all the union republics were parts of the unified budget of the USSR. As regards participation by foreign States in investment activity, that was not possible.

The definition used in the FPInvA is consequently directed towards the state of affairs which existed prior to the commencement of perestroika and is a manifestation of a clear conservative trend.

4.   Point 2 of this Article promises a theoretical classification of the grounds on which investment activity rests. But the promise is not fulfilled. The FPInvA affirms that investment activity is effectuated on the basis of ... investing. A distinction between investing and investment activity is hardly evident. In any event, it is impossible to structure a classification of the types of investment activity by delimiting the types of investing.

5.   The list set out in Point 2 of this Article has a certain legal significance. It is linked with the description of one aspect of the investment market which was incorporated in Article 1, paragraph one. There the FPInvA, using economic categories, described one aspect as "all types of property and intellectual valuables." Here the FPInvA moves on to the language of law and characterises this aspect juridically from the standpoint of the subjects which possess such valuables.

The FPInvA singles out four groups of such subjects. Three of them are named, but the first is not. The FPInvA included subjects so distinct from one another that finding a common name for them was not possible.

Citizens are first named in the FPInvA as a group. This is fully in the spirit of perestroika. In the past citizens were treated by the law primarily as participants of relations relating to personal consumption and legislation was concerned principally with the satisfaction of their material and cultural requirements. The FPInvA begins the list of subjects with citizens, who may function in the future investment market. The financial prerequisites for this exist. Suffice it to say that the total deposits owned by citizens in the Savings Bank of the USSR exceeded 400 billion rubles. According to some estimates, the populace holds more than 100 billion rubles additionally in cash.

More complicated is the question of the legal prerequisites. The FPInvA named citizens first, but legislative acts adopted long before the FPInvA have a restrained attitude towards citizens as potential investors. The Statute on Joint-Stock Societies confirmed by the USSR Council of Ministers on 19 June 1991 allows citizens to be among the participants of joint-stock societies. But there is a reservation which is not made with respect to other participants: "unless provided otherwise by legislative acts of the USSR and the union and autonomous republics" (point 3).[12] Moreover, citizens have been deprived of the right to be possessors of bearer stocks (point 34).

In practice at the end of 1990 the first steps were taken to involve citizens in investing. The stocks of a commercial investment bank, the "Menatepinvest" joint-stock society, and the "Menatep" Trade House were offered to the public.[13]

---

[12]   Translated in W. E. Butler (ed.), *Basic Documents on the Soviet Legal System* (2d ed., 1991), pp. 323-344.

Non-State enterprises are next mentioned in the FPInvA. This concept has not been used in other all-union laws, and here is doubtless being used as a euphemism for private enterprises. There has been a sharp debate in the Soviet Union as to whether private entrepreneurship should be allowed. The FPInvA treaded lightly around the controversy by selecting a neutral expression.

Next the FPInvA enumerates juridical persons based on collective ownership. The list of such juridical persons was laid down in the 1990 USSR Law on Ownership.[14] In addition to those enumerated in the FPInvA, there are cooperatives, joint-stock societies, collective enterprises, and also, at least in part, lease enterprises.

The second group of investors singled out by the FPInvA are combined together under the denomination of State investing. There are in fact two types of investors: agencies of power and administration, and State enterprises and institutions. Budget assets are the source of finance for the first type, although extrabudgetary funds have a certain role, as do borrowed assets. The source of investments for State enterprises is their own assets and loans.

Budget assets are still the principal source for investment finance in the Soviet Union. Therefore the principal investors are the agencies of power and administration at all levels of the State pyramid: the USSR, union republics, autonomous republics, autonomous national areas and regions, territories, regions, districts, and other administrative-territorial formations.

---

[13]   *Pravda*, 28 December 1990, p. 6.

[14]   See M. I. Braginskii, W. E. Butler, and A. A. Rubanov (commentary), *The Law on Ownership in the USSR* (1991) pp. 51-67.

The status of a State enterprise as an investor is determined by the fact that in accordance with the 1990 USSR Law on Ownership, the property which is in State ownership and allocated to a State enterprise belongs to it by right of full economic jurisdiction. That Law provides that in effectuating the right of full economic jurisdiction over its property an enterprise possesses, uses, and disposes of the said property and at its discretion performs any transactions with respect to it which are not contrary to law (Article 24[1]). By virtue of this rule a State enterprise has the right to also perform transactions needed for investing the assets which belong to it.

A State institution is in a different position. It is on the State budget, whose assets are not in its full economic jurisdiction. And the 1990 USSR Law on Ownership provides that State institutions or organisations on the State budget which might in the instances provided for by legislative acts of the USSR and the union and autonomous republics effectuate economic activity shall acquire the right to autonomous disposition of revenues from such activity and property acquired from those revenues (Article 26[2]). Those revenues or property also are the financial base for the participation of State institutions and organisations as investors.

The third group of investors falls into the concept of foreign investing. It includes foreign citizens, foreign juridical persons, and foreign States. This is an especially vital clarification of the rule set out in Article 1, paragraph one, which was based on economic rather than legal principles and said nothing of the national affiliation of the valuables. Here the FPInvA establishes that valuables also function in the investment market, the right to which are possessed by subjects belonging to other States. Those subjects participate as potential investors also in foreign capital markets. The FPInvA thus sanctions the link of market investments which might be made in the USSR with the foreign capital market.

The Soviet Union has an enormous need for foreign investment. According to private estimates, the national economy of the Russian Federation alone should have $90 billion invested in it from abroad.[15] The rate of growth of foreign investment, pending the enactment of foreign investment and pledge legislation, has been slow. Some observers believe that if one accepts the correlation of accumulated foreign capital investment against gross national product at the rate of 2-3% (which is twice lower than the average level for developed countries and three times lower than third world countries), foreign juridical persons should invest at a minimum $30 billion of direct investments in the Soviet economy.[16]

The fourth group set out in the FPInvA engages in joint investing, by which is meant not only those situations in which several investors are affiliated with different States, but also where the investors have a common nationality affiliation but different forms of ownership.

6.   The list of groups of investors is exhaustive. And although in all four groups many various subjects have been named, there remains nonetheless a significant gap. The FPInv overlooked international inter-State organisations.

International inter-State organisations do not fall within any of the varieties of investors named by the

---

[15]   *Kommersant*, no. 12 (1991) p. 7

[16]   *Ekonomika i zhizn'*, no. 46 (1990) p. 20.

FPInvA. They are, of course, distinct from States. The theory of public international law recognises States to be the principal subjects of international law, whereas international inter-State organisations are derivative subjects of international law. The latter also do not fall within the category of foreign juridical persons. They are not juridical persons, but subjects of international law.

The silence of the FPInvA regarding investing by international inter-State organisations placed the Soviet Union, juridically speaking, outside an important channel for receiving investments. Organisations of this type which are large investors exist in the world. And the position was the more complicated because the Soviet Union has considerable interests linked with investment activity by certain international inter-State organisations (see Commentary to Article 4[1]). The gap finally was repaired on with the enactment on 5 July 1991 of the FPForInv, which included "international organisations" amongst the list of foreign investors.[17]

7. The FPInvA confines itself in this Article to a legal characterisation of investors. But no attempt is made in this Article or any other to use the language of the law to characterise the recipients of investments. Given the effort of the FPInvA to develop a theoretical design for investment, one might have expected it to undertake a classification of the recipients of investments as well.

This has not happened. The FPInvA took a one-sided approach to investment activity. Other participants of investment activity fall within its range, but not the recipients of investments. For the latter the FPInvA offers only one method: a description in economic terms as to

[17]   Reproduced as Annexe 3 herein

what are the objects of entrepreneurial (or other) activity (see Commentary to Article 1).

It would be possible to classify recipients of investments. For example, it is not only possible but indeed essential to differentiate between internal and external investing because the FPInvA refers to this in Article 5 (see Commentary to Article 5[2] and [4]). However, a classification along these lines inevitably would lead to distinguishing between investments received by State objects and investments directed towards the non-State sector, and within those categories, to investments whose recipients are private entrepreneurs. The FPInvA named citizens in the first group of investors. Logic requires that they be named among the first group of recipients of investments. But the FPInvA does not do so.

Article 3: Objects of Investment Activity

Newly created and modernised basic funds and circulating assets in all branches and spheres of the national economy, securities, special purpose monetary deposits, scientific-technical products, intellectual valuables, other objects of ownership, as well as property rights, shall be objects of investment activity.

Investing in objects, the creation and use of which does not meet the requirements of sanitary-hygienic, ecological, and other norms established by legislation of the USSR and the union and autonomous republics, as well as causing damage to the rights and interests protected by law of citizens, juridical persons, and a State, shall be prohibited.

1.   There is an inconsistency between the title of this Article and its content. According to its title, the Article should define the concept of an object of investment activity. Such a definition would have been in the spirit of the FPInvA effort to achieve theoretical respectability and consistent with the arrangement of the Articles to follow a scheme borrowed from elementary legal textbooks: "activity -- object -- subject" (see Commentary to Article 1).

Whereas in Article 1 of the FPInvA a definition of investment activity is given, in this Article the legislator refrains from offering a definition of object of investment activity. Neither the first nor the second paragraphs of this Article disclose what such an object is. The second paragraph defines what it is not, whereas the first gives an exemplary list instead of a definition.

The legislator should not be reproached for being unwilling to act extemporaneously. The object of relations which arise in the sphere of investment activity is a question which requires scholarly research. Already it may be foreseen that there will not be a simple answer. It would have been premature to offer a legislative definition of an object in the FPInvA.

The list is no substitute for a definition. The problem is that the list in paragraph one of this Article coincides almost completely with the list given in Article 1. All the phenomena named in Article 3 already had been specified in Article 1, except for circulating funds and objects of ownership not already mentioned.

Repetition in and of itself does not embellish a law. It is even worse when identical phenomena in the FPInvA are classified differently. Securities, for example, special-purpose bank deposits, and intellectual valuables are called investments in Article 1, but in this Article are called objects of investment activity. Basic funds in Article 1 figure as recipients of investments, whereas here they are objects of investment activity. Abstractly, they might be regarded as having both aspects. But in legislation pursuing the aim of creating the precise legal regulation of relations, this is not acceptable. It is difficult to avoid the impression that in issues close to the domain of legal theory the legislator is engaged in circular reasoning.

2. The rules contained in Article 3, paragraph two, deserve great attention. They are an important addition to the provisions of the FPInvA concerning the potential recipients of investments as objects of entrepreneurship or other activity. Whereas previously the FPInvA characterised the recipient in broad economic terms (see

Commentary to Article 1), here the legislator limits significantly the sphere of operation of this broad rule.

It should be noted above all that the FPInvA uses a rather sharply-worded expression: "investing ... shall be prohibited." The expression "shall be prohibited" is rarely used in civil-law legislation.

The FPInvA provided for three categories of violations which entail a prohibition of investing. Investments are not permitted in those objects whose creation and use: (1) does not meet the requirements of legal norms specified in the FPInvA; (2) causes harm to rights and interests protected by law; and (3) causes harm to subjects specified in the FPInvA.

3.   As regards the first prohibition, it should be noted that the list of legal norms which investments must satisfy has been broadly drawn and is not specific. The FPInvA provides that the creation and use of an object must meet not only sanitary-hygienic and ecological requirements, but also other norms established by legislation of the USSR and the union and autonomous republics. The reference to sanitary-hygienic and ecological norms is wholly justified. Compliance with those requirements does not create insuperable obstacles for investing, although precisely what "ecological" norms are also requires some clarification. For the most part such rules are established by the State Committee for Construction and Investments of the USSR.

The reference to "other norms" is another matter. The FPInvA does not indicate what kind of rules it has in view. Perhaps the formulation includes all legal norms affecting the creation and use of objects of investing except the sanitary-hygienic and ecological rules. Further, the

FPInvA could be indicating "other rules" adopted at the all-union and republic levels of legislation, or even local administrative-territorial entities. In essence, the FPInvA has prohibited investments in objects whose creation and use does not meet the requirements of any norm of Soviet law.

This provision of the FPInvA counteracts the movement of the Soviet economy towards the market. For the investment market to function normally it is essential that legislation clearly and precisely establish which norms of law determine the admissibility of investing. The reference of the FPInvA to "other norms" places potential investors, especially foreign investors, in a difficult position, for it presupposes the detailed study in advance of the entire complex of Soviet legal norms which might have some relevance to the creation and use of the object of the contemplated investment.

It should be noted that the reference to "other norms" might serve under Article 20(3) of the FPInvA as the basis for a State agency to exercise its right to render a decision to terminate or suspend investment activity if in the process of effectuating it a determination is made that its continuance will lead to a violation of norms established by legislation. Not only sanitary-hygienic or ecological norms, but also "other norms."

4. The second grounds for the prohibition of investments is the causing of harm by the creation and use of the object to the rights and interests of citizens protected by law. This prohibition also has been formulated too broadly, and it too is capable of counteracting the movement towards the market economy.

Legislation protects a vast range of rights and interests of citizens. It follows from the FPInvA that for a prohibition to be relevant is suffices to create or use an object which would cause harm to any one of those rights and interests. This also places the potential investor in an impossible position. In deciding to invest, he must be familiar with the vast range of legal rights and interests of citizens which might one way or another be adversely affected by the construction or operation of the respective object. Again an extensive and comprehensive analysis of the specific legal situation is essential.

It also must be noted that the FPInvA does not require that these rights and interests be necessarily violated by the creation and use of the object. It suffices that they simply be harmed. Harm may not ensue without a violation of rights and interests. For example, it may be contemplated to invest in an operating enterprise for the purpose of creating a new completely automated shop within it. The right to labour of workers who are employed in the old shop, protected by law (Article 40, USSR Constitution) is not violated by this. But they may be harmed, that is, the workers will have to exercise their right to labour at a new place of work.

5.   The third basis for prohibiting investment is the causing of harm by the creation or use of an object to the subjects specified in the FPInvA. Among those subjects, the first-named are juridical persons. The FPInvA establishes that investment is prohibited in objects "the creation and use of which ... cause damage to ... juridical persons ..."

It should be emphasised that it is sufficient for a prohibition that the creation and use of the object caused damage to a juridical person. The FPInvA says nothing about a violation of rights or a violation of the legally protected interests of the juridical person. It suffices that the juridical person is harmed, irrespective of whether his rights and legally-protected interests are violated or not.

In a market economy this provision of the FPInvA would sharply limit competition. Any juridical person who produces any product on the Soviet market or offers any services is harmed if as a result of the investment a competitor appears in the market. This competitor does not violate any rights of the juridical person, but the appearance in the market of his products or services, of course, caused harm to this juridical person. The latter, relying on this provision of the FPInvA, would have the opportunity to attempt to prohibit the investment.

This provision of the FPInvA discloses the true attitude of the enactment towards the market. The Preamble states that it is directed towards ensuring the effective functioning of the national economy under the conditions of a market economy. The development and maintenance of competition is an essential element of the market economy. The norm being considered is clearly directed towards limiting competition. It helps juridical persons already present in the future market to create a monopoly position for themselves, even though certain provisions of the FPInvA also mention anti-monopoly measures (see for example Article 11).

One may imagine that Article 3, paragraph two, is somehow skewed. Perhaps the legislator should have written that investing is prohibited when it causes harm to the *rights* of juridical persons. There is some basis to so suppose. Article 20, point 3, establishes that the decision of a State agency to terminate or suspend investments may be adopted "if in the process of investment activity it is elicited that its continuation will lead to a violation of ... the rights and interests of ... juridical persons ..." Here it is not sufficient to terminate for simply causing damage to a juridical person.

But this is merely a presupposition. The FPInvA has actually provided that "investing shall be prohibited in objects whose creation and use ... cause damage ... to juridical persons" (Article 3, paragraph two).

6. The FPInvA also establishes that investing is prohibited in objects "whose creation and use ... causes damage to ... the State." As in the case of juridical persons, there is no requirement here that rights or interests legally protected by the State be violated. It suffices that damage be caused to the State.

In accordance with the USSR Constitution, the State is the USSR and the union and autonomous republics. This provision of the FPInvA ensures to each of them the possibility of creating a monopoly position in the future market. One must bear in mind that States are the dominant subjects of the Soviet economy. According to the 1990 USSR Law on Ownership, the major pipelines are in all-union ownership, as are the unified electric power system of the USSR, space systems, and all-union communications and information systems (Article 21). The union republics have enterprises and national-economic complexes in their ownership, as well as higher educational institutions, and others (Article 22). Autonomous republics own agricultural, domestic servicing, transport, industrial, construction, and other enterprises, complexes, and the like (Article 22).[18]

---

[18]   See M. I. Braginskii, W. E. Butler, and A. A. Rubanov (commentary), *The Law on Ownership in the USSR* (1991).

This enumeration shows how extensive is the range of instances when this provision of the FPInvA might be applied. It may be argued that the intent of the FPInvA was not adequately expressed. Article 20(3) speaks merely about the rights and interests of the State protected by law. But this likewise is merely a presupposition. The text reads: "Investing shall be prohibited in objects whose creation and use ... causes damage ... to the State (Article 3, paragraph two)

Article 4: Subjects of Investment Activity

1. Soviet and foreign citizens, juridical persons, and States may be subjects (investors and participants) of investment activity.

2. Investors shall be subjects of investment activity who take decisions on the investment of their own, borrowed, or attracted property and intellectual valuables.

Investors may act in the role of contributors, creditors, or purchasers, as well as fulfil the functions of any participant of investment activity.

3. Soviet and foreign citizens and juridical persons ensuring the effectuation of investments as executors of orders or on the basis of the commission of an investor shall be participants of investment activity.

1. In continuing to follow the civil law textbooks (see Commentary to Article 1), the FPInvA in point 1 of this Article have again attempted to achieve a certain theoretical respectability by raising the question of who may be a subject of investment activity. Following their practice in Article 2 (see Commentary to Article 2), where they substituted a definition of investment activity for a definition of the relations connected with effectuating investment activity, here they speak not of the subjects of relations regulated by legislation on investments, but rather about the subjects of investment activity.

The allocation of a separate article to such subjects has indicated that the FPInvA is in fact unable to formulate an appropriate definition. A proper definition would require the identification of indicia which would distinguish such subjects from participants in any other activity. That would be a task of enormous complexity. The civil law textbooks, when they are able to offer such definitions, have many years of research work to back their conclusions. The FPInvA has nothing whatever to rest upon. Either it offers extemporaneous propositions or it offers a list in place of a definition.

The FPInvA in the end favoured a list, which is certainly preferable to an impromptu definition. But the list casts no light on the theoretical conception from which the law proceeded and raises suspicion that indeed there was no conceptual position developed.

The FPInvA understands investment activity to be the aggregate actions relating to the realisation of investments, and investments are all types of property and intellectual valuables (see Commentary to Article 2[1]). Under such an approach the list must be so drawn that it embraces all subjects of all activity relating to the realisation of all types of valuables.

The FPInvA has named the subjects of investment activity as citizens, juridical persons, and States, both Soviet and foreign. But this method of enumerating subjects conceals the threat that someone is overlooked, and indeed the FPInvA here erred by not including international inter-State organisations and stateless persons. The former is especially serious since certain international financial organisations carry on extensive investment operations (see Commentary to Article 4[1]) the omission was repaired by including "international organisations" in the 1991 FPForInv.

But at the same time the list of subjects of investment activity is so broad that it cannot delimit investment activity from other types of activity which subjects engage in. It is true that Soviet and foreign citizens participate in investment activity, as do juridical persons and States. But they are subjects of many other types of activity, including industrial, trade, or transport activities.

2.   The list of subjects of investment activity in point 1 of this Article is repetitive of another provision in the FPInvA and therefore circular. Article 2(1) already provided that investment activity is understood to be the aggregate of practical actions of citizens, juridical persons, and States. The FPInvA already has indicated thereby who is a subject of investment activity. To repeat this in another Article is merely to hold on to a scheme having pretensions to theoretical respectability and risks a directly contrary result.

3.   The FPInvA divides subjects of investment activity into investors and participants of investment activity. That distinction is yet another extemporaneous invention of the legislator and has never been discussed in doctrinal writings. This distinction is clearly unsuccessful. It follows from it that an investor is not a participant in investment activity. In recognising the investor as a subject of investment activity, the FPInvA simultaneously does not recognise him as a participant thereof, a strange view of the investor indeed. The FPInvA assumes the investor is a passive figure who, though involved in the process of

investing, somehow can not claim the role of a participant in investment activity.

This view is inconsistent with the FPInvA itself, which speaks of the investor in other provisions as quite an active figure. The FPInvA provides, for example, that the investor determines the amounts, orientations, and effectiveness of the investments made and attracts the juridical and natural persons needed to realise the investments (Article 6[2]). The investor obtains the requisite authorisations and agreements for capital construction and expert opinions regarding the investment projects (Article 8[1]). These and numerous other provisions of the FPInvA regarding the investor do not support the view of him as a person who is not a participant of investment activity.

4. The list of subjects of investment activity contained in Article 4(1) begins with Soviet citizens. Under a market economy this is the proper approach because such an economy presupposes the extensive participation of citizens in the investment markets. But, as noted, there exist serious financial obstacles to citizen involvement. The public is believed to hold about 500 billion rubles in savings banks and in cash. But attracting those funds to the investment market has proceeded very slowly, although the privatisation programme is beginning to gather momentum.

Individuals have become more aware of and interested in investment opportunities. The sale of stocks issued by Zapaduralbank (Perm Region) in April 1991 brought 150,000 rubles. The general public in the Perm Region hold more than three billion rubles in the Savings Bank of the USSR and have been restrained in their investment activity. However, after the official increases in prices during Spring 1991, their behaviour has changed markedly.[19]

5. The State is placed last on the list, a positioning that accords with the state of affairs in the capital markets in market-economy countries. But the fact that the FPInvA devotes all of Section III to the State is not consistent with its true role in the capital markets, and indeed other subjects of investment activity enumerated in this Article before the State are not given commensurate attention.

The State today is the principal investor. Enormous sums pass through the channels of budget investment. According to some sources, State investments amount to one-third of national income.[20] By spring 1991, however, State investment had passed from the stage of crisis to one of veritable anarchy. In 1990 uncompleted construction exceeded the normative standards by more than 25 billion rubles.[21] Of the 505 objects of a production character whose construction was included in the 1990 State Order, only 155 were accepted into operation. In 1989 241 objects included in the State Order fell through as not completed, and in 1990 103 still had not been introduced into operation.[22] The grave economic situation has temporarily suspended the construction of many production objects. In 1989 there were 24,500 such objects with an estimate value of 29.5 billion rubles.[23] One such object was the construction of a tractor plant in Elabug; while it was

[19]   *Kommersant*, no. 14 (1991) p. 7.

[20]   *Izvestiia*, 30 October 1990, p. 2.

[21]   *Izvestiia*, 20 December 1990, p. 10.

[22]   *Izvestiia*, 25 January 1991, p. 4.

[23]   *Izvestiia*, 24 January 1991, p. 4.

being built, a decision was taken to transform it into an automobile plant. More than one billion rubles already had been invested in the construction, but there was no indication that it would ever be completed.[24]

The prospects for State investing are rather murky. The 1991 Union budget contains no assets for capital investment in new construction.[25] According to some predictions, the total capital investment in 1991 would decrease by 15.5% in comparison with 1990 in the national economy as a whole and by 28.7% in the production sphere.

There also is an inconsistency in the norms which relate to the State. It follows from point 1 of this Article that the State might be both an investor and a "participant of investment activity." However, according to point 3 of this Article the State may not be a "participant of investment activity."

6. The FPInvA names among the subjects of investment activity foreign juridical persons. This means that a foreign juridical person is capable of being what the FPInvA calls a "participant of foreign investment activity." It follows that the capacity to be an investor is recognised for a foreign juridical person.

This provision of the FPInvA is of principled significance. Until recently there were no normative acts in the Soviet Union recognising that foreign juridical persons enjoyed such capacity. It was said for the first time in the Edict of the President of the USSR of 26 October 1990 on foreign investments in the USSR.[26] But a presidential edict

---

[24]   See the Statement by Chairman of Gosstroi in *Izvestiia*, 30 October 1990, p. 2.

[25]   *Izvestiia*, 30 December 1990, p. 3.

is not a law. The FPInvA was the first law adopted by the USSR Supreme Soviet to state this position.

To appreciate this, one must recall that Soviet law traditionally has been very restrained towards foreign juridical persons, and this was reflected especially in that such persons were acknowledged to have merely one role in foreign economic relations: that of a potential partner of Soviet organisations with respect to foreign trade transactions.

For seventy years a system of authorisations operated in Soviet civil law for foreign juridical persons. The 1922 RSFSR Civil Code had provided that foreign joint-stock societies, partnerships and others acquire the rights of a juridical person in the RSFSR only with the special authorisation of the government (see Article 8, Note 1, of the Introductory Law of the RSFSR Civil Code). Later an all-union law of the same type was published. The Decree of the Central Executive Committee and Council of People's Commissars of 11 March 1931 "On the Procedure for Admitting Foreign Firms to the Performance of Trade Operations on the Territory of the USSR" provided that foreign trade and industrial organisations are allowed to perform trade operations in the USSR only by special authorisation.[27]

A foreign juridical person which had not received such authorisation was regarded in the USSR as, if not nonexistent, then in any event as having a limited range of rights. The 1922 RSFSR Civil Code, for example, merely

---

[26]   *Vedomosti SND SSSR* (1990) no. 44, item 944; transl. in M. I. Braginskii, W. E. Butler, and A. A. Rubanov (commentary), *The Law on Ownership in the USSR* (1991) pp. 311-313; and reproduced herein as Annex 2

[27]   *SZ SSSR* (1931) item 197, transl. in V. V. Gsovski, *Soviet Civil Law* (1949) II, pp. 343-346.

gave a juridical person the right to legal protection with regard to claims against defendants situated in the RSFSR.

The law recognised for foreign juridical persons only the role of potential partners of Soviet organisations with regard to foreign trade transactions, for which in this case a departure from the authorisation procedure was allowed. The Decree of 11 March 1931 provided that foreign organisations need not obtain an authorisation when concluding individual transactions relating to foreign trade with foreign trade associations of the USSR (Article 12). This exception also was confirmed later. The 1961 FPCivL provided that "Foreign enterprises and organisations may perform in the USSR without special authorisation transactions relating to foreign trade and account, insurance, and other operations connected therewith with Soviet foreign trade associations and other Soviet organisations to whom the right to perform such transactions has been granted."[28] Such language has been completely eliminated from the 1991 FPCivL.

7.   In early 1987 the first indications appeared that the Soviet legislator was rethinking the role which foreign juridical persons should play in the foreign economic turnover of the Soviet Union. The Decree of the USSR Council of Ministers of 13 January 1987, No. 49, on the procedure for creating joint enterprises in the Soviet Union granted to foreign juridical persons the right to be co-founders of joint enterprises.[29] This was the first step outside the framework of their traditional role of partners

---

[28]   Article 124. Translated in W. E. Butler, *The Soviet Legal System: Legislation and Documentation* (1978) p. 427. On this system generally, see Butler, *Soviet Law* (2d ed., 1988) pp. 378-394.

[29]   Transl. in W. E. Butler (ed.), *Basic Documents on the Soviet Legal Syste* (2d ed., 1991), pp. 475-484.

of Soviet organisations under foreign trade contracts. The legal system began to view them as potential investors, although within limits.

Joint enterprises with the participation of Soviet and foreign juridical persons are presently the principal form of foreign investments in the USSR. More than 3400 joint enterprises have been registered, although less than one-third are actually operating and fewer than fifty in the production sphere. The process of creating joint enterprises has slowed, partly because Soviet participants lack foreign currency assets to invest.

Since 1987 the decree on joint enterprises has been amended on several occasions. For the most part these changes represented a liberalisation. At the outset, for example, it was stipulated that the share of the Soviet participant must be not less than 51%. At present the share of the participants is determined by agreement between them. Initially joint enterprises were created only with the authorisation of the USSR Council of Ministers. Now such decisions are taken by State enterprises with the consent of the superior agencies of administration. In the beginning the chairman of the board and general director of a joint enterprise had to be citizens of the USSR. Now foreign citizens may hold those positions.

Another direction in legislative change has been to enlarge the instances when a joint enterprise functioning in the economy would be equated to ordinary participants of civil turnover. It was initially established that deliveries to a joint enterprise from the Soviet market of equipment, raw materials, materials, fuel, energy, and the like must be effectuated only through the Soviet foreign trade organisations. Presently joint enterprises are incorporated in the general system of planned material-technical supply in the USSR.[30]

In certain instances joint enterprises received the rights which Soviet enterprises did not have (for example, the right to autonomously determine in what currency accounts would be settled for products obtained from the Soviet market). And in a few cases there was regression: an example is the procedure introduced whereby a joint enterprise required authorisation to engage in middleman operations relating to export and import.

Substantial changes have occurred with regard to the forms in which joint enterprises might be created.

When Decree No. 49 was adopted on 13 January 1987, Soviet law differed materially with regard to the form of enterprises from the majority of foreign legal systems. It lacked rules defining in general terms what forms an enterprise might take. In the 1920s there were such rules in the RSFSR Civil Code, but they had been repealed. In their place differentiating rules were introduced devoted to individual types of enterprises. Some rules appertained to State enterprises, and others to cooperatives, and yet others to collective farms, and so on. There were no general provisions on the form of enterprises.

Decree No. 49 introduced a new type of enterprise, called joint enterprises, but was unable to apply to them any norms of a general character defining the form of enterprises. The Decree itself was obliged to set out detailed rules regulating this new form.

The 1990 USSR Law on Ownership established that joint enterprises may be created in the form of joint-stock societies, and also in the form of economic societies and

---

[30]   For details, see A. A. Rubanov, "Pravovoe regulirovanie snabzheniia i sbyta sovmestnykh predpriiatii s uchastiem zapadnykh firm v usloviiakh formirovaniia rynka," *Pravovoe regulirovanie rynochnykh otnoshenii v SSSR* (1980) pp. 76-88.

partnerships (Article 27).[31] Somewhat later there also appeared rules regulating the respective forms.

On 19 June 1990 the USSR Council of Ministers confirmed the Statute on Joint-Stock Societies and Limited Responsibility Societies.[32] Legislation on joint-stock societies also appeared in individual republics. Amongst them, the RSFSR Council of Ministers on 25 December 1990 confirmed a republic Statute on Joint-Stock Societies. There were considerable differences between the all-union and RSFSR acts as regards foreign juridical persons. The USSR Statute provided that only Soviet juridical persons and citizens might be founders of a joint-stock society (point 38) but further stipulated that "The peculiarities of participation of foreign juridical persons and citizens in joint-stock and limited responsibility societies shall be determined by legislative acts of the USSR and the union and autonomous republics" (point 1). The legislation adopted in the RSFSR, on the contrary, provided that "foreign juridical ... persons may also act in the role of founders in accordance with legislation on foreign investments" (point 11).[33] It further stipulates that "societies with the participation of foreign juridical ... persons shall be registered by the RSFSR Ministry of Finances in accordance with the present Statute and prevailing legislation of the RSFSR on foreign investments" (point 31).

8.   The appearance of legislation on joint enterprises was an important advance in Soviet law with respect to the role of foreign juridical persons in Soviet economic life.

---

[31]   M. I. Braginskii, W. E. Butler, and A. A. Rubanov (commentary), *The Law on Ownership in the USSR* (1991) pp. 243-253.

[32]   Transl. in W. E. Butler (ed.), *Basic Documents on the Soviet Legal System* (2d ed., 1991) pp. 323-344.

[33]   *SP RSFSR* (1991), no. 6, item 92.

However, this new view of their role in polished form only penetrated into legislation somewhat later. Of importance in this connection is the Edict of the President of the USSR of 26 October 1990 on foreign investments in the USSR.[34] Thereafter Soviet law regarded foreign juridical persons not only as partners of Soviet organisations in foreign trade transactions, but also as potential investors.

The Edict provided that foreign juridical persons may create on the territory of the USSR enterprises in which foreign investments comprise 100% of the property (Article 2). Such enterprises are juridical persons under Soviet legislation.

The Edict opened for foreign juridical persons the possibility of using all forms of enterprises permitted by Soviet legislation and that enterprises with foreign investments are created in any forms permitted by USSR and republic legislation. Enabling legislation exists for three such forms: the joint-stock society, limited responsibility society, and small enterprise.[35] Also mentioned in Soviet legislation are Kommandit partnerships, partnerships, and one-man companies.

Some foreign juridical persons took advantage of the new opportunities at once. Within several days after the Edict was issued, two wholly foreign-owned enterprises were registered, one as a joint-stock society and the other as a small enterprise.

The Edict of 26 October 1990 provided for three ways by which a foreign juridical person might effectuate investments. First, by share participation in enterprises

---

[34] *Vedomosti SND SSSR* (1990) no. 44, item 944; transl. in M. I. Braginskii, W. E. Butler, and A. A. Rubanov (commentary), *The Law on Ownership in the USSR* (1991) pp. 311-313; and reproduced as Annexe 2 herein

[35] *SP SSSR* (1990) no. 19, item 101.

organised jointly with Soviet juridical persons and citizens; second, by the acquisition of property, stocks, and other securities; and third, by acquiring either autonomously or with the participation of Soviet juridical persons and citizens the right to use land and other property rights, including the acquisition of rights under a long-term lease (in accordance with USSR and republic legislation). To this the 1991 FPForInv have added a fourth way: the creation of enterprises belonging wholly to the investors.

The Edict also defined the basic principles of the legal status of enterprises created by foreign juridical persons either autonomously or with Soviet juridical persons and citizens: "... their regime may not be less favourable than the respective regime for the property of Soviet enterprises, organisations, and citizens" (Article 3). This provision is of great practical importance because enterprises with foreign participation operate in an unusual economic milieu. In any event, joint enterprises have come against serious difficulties as regards the supply of raw materials and the like.[36]

The founding and the activities of enterprises created by foreign juridical persons has been facilitated by the provision of the Presidential Edict which stipulates that profits of foreign investors received in the Soviet Union in Soviet currencymay be freely reinvested and used on the territory of the USSR in accordance with USSR and republic legislation, and also transferred abroad in the procedure established by legislation of the USSR.

Finally, the Edict provided that "foreign investments on the territory of the USSR shall enjoy legal protection ..." (Article 3).

---

[36] See A. A. Rubanov, "Sovmestnoe predpriiatie s uchastiem zapadnykh firm kak sub"ekt khoziaistvennoi deiatel'nosti," in *Sovmestnye predpriiatii: sozdanie i deiatel'nost'* (1990), pp. 47-53.

The Edict of 26 October 1990 has been a major factor in changing the views of Soviet law regarding the role of foreign juridical persons in the economic life of the Soviet Union. But it should be borne in mind that the USSR Constitution, as amended, gives to the President of the USSR the right to issue edicts on the basis of and in execution of provisions of the Constitution itself and laws of the USSR (Article 127-5). When the Edict was issued on 26 October 1990, neither the USSR Constitution nor a USSR law contained provisions establishing that foreign juridical persons could act as investors. The 1990 USSR Law on Ownership established merely that foreign juridical persons have the right to have in ownership in the USSR in industrial and other enterprises, buildings, installations, and other property for the purposes of effectuating economic and other activities (see Article 29).[37]

The FPInvA was the first law in which a new view of the role of foreign juridical persons in the Soviet economy was expressed, the legislator expressly acknowledging them to be investors.

Neither the FPInvA nor the Presidential Edict regulated all questions which arise in connection with foreign investments. The foundation enactment is the 1991 FPForInv and concomitant republic foreign investment laws.[38]

9. The FPInvA names foreign citizens as being among the subjects of investment activity. They fall into

---

[37]   See M. I. Braginskii, W. E. Butler, and A. A. Rubanov (commentary), *The Law on Ownership in the USSR* (1991), pp. 271-278.

[38]   Among them, the 1991 Kazakh Law on Foreign Investments and the 1990 Lithuanian Law on Foreign Investments. The 1991 FPForInv is reproduced as Annexe 3.

the category not only of those whom the FPInvA calls a "participant of investment activity," but also investors.

The attitude of Soviet law towards the role of foreign citizens in the Soviet economy has undergone an even more complex evolution than that with regard to foreign juridical persons. At the outset Soviet law recognised various roles for foreign citizens depending upon whether they had an enterprise outside the USSR or not. If they did not, foreign citizens were regarded as ordinary participants in day-to-day life whose relations were regulated by civil law rules. The legal regime of foreign citizens in the USSR thus from the very beginning was composed of three elements. The principal one was the principle of equating foreign citizens and citizens of the USSR. The second comprised individual exceptions from the principle of equalisation. And in certain cases the law further endowed foreign citizens with rights not enjoyed by Soviet citizens.

The principle of equalisation is expressed in a number of legislative acts and extends to all foreign citizens irrespective of whether they are resident on the territory of the USSR or abroad. The USSR Law of 24 June 1981 "On the Legal Status of Foreign Citizens in the USSR" provides that "Foreign citizens in the USSR shall enjoy the same rights and freedoms and bear the same duties as citizens of the USSR, unless it follows otherwise from the USSR Constitution, the present Law, and other acts of Soviet legislation."[39] The 1991 FPCivL provides, in a narrower context, that "Foreign citizens and stateless persons shall enjoy civil legal capacity in the USSR on an equal basis with Soviet citizens" (Article 160).[40]

---

[39]   Article 3, para. one. *Vedomosti SSSR* (1981) no. 26, item 836; transl. in W. E. Butler (transl. & ed.), *Basic Documents on the Soviet Legal System* (1983), p. 257.

[40]   W. E. Butler (intro. & transl.), *The USSR Fundamental Principles of Civil Legislation* (1991).

The second element of the legal regime of foreign citizens -- the individual limitations of rights in comparison with Soviet citizens -- is a departure from the principle of equalisation in the bad sense of the word. Such limitations are few in number and do not play a determinative role in the legal regime of foreign citizens. There are two types of such limitations, both found in the FPCivL. Article 160 of the FPCivL having established that foreign citizens and stateless persons enjoy rights on an equal basis, it goes on to stipulate that "individual exceptions may be established by legislative acts of the USSR" (Article 160). Such exceptions are not numerous.

The second type of limitation may be established by way of reprisal. The FPCivL provides that "Retaliatory limitations with respect to citizens of those States in which there are special limitations on the legal capacity of Soviet citizens may be established by the Government of the USSR" (Article 162). However, no such limitations have been introduced.

The third element of the legal regime of foreign citizens is rights which only they may possess and which Soviet citizens may not. These are what might be called desirable departures from the principle of equalisation. Such departures also are few in number.

As regards foreign citizens who own an enterprise outside the USSR, Soviet law began by recognising their role as potential partners of Soviet organisations in foreign trade transactions. During the 1920-30s, there were a number of individual merchants in nearby countries who maintained active trade relations with the USSR. Consequently, the Decree of 11 March 1931 on the procedure for admitting foreign firms for the performance of trade operations on the territory of the USSR specially mentioned foreign citizens as possible participants of foreign trade transactions (Article 12).[41]

Thereafter special provisions of this type disappeared from legislative acts, principally because individual merchants became less significant in neighbouring countries. The 1961 FPCivL omitted any mention of foreign citizens as possible participants of foreign trade transactions with Soviet organisations; only foreign enterprises and organisations were stipulated.[42] Soviet law consequently came to regard foreign citizens merely as the subjects of relations arising in day-to-day life, such as copyright, inheritance, and the like.

From early 1990 a new trend emerged in Soviet law. Foreign citizens began to be recognised as potential investors. The first step was the provision of the 1990 USSR Law on Ownership, which provided that foreign citizens had the right to create joint enterprises in the USSR with Soviet juridical persons (Article 27).[43]

It is of interest that the advance with respect to natural persons occurred somewhat later than with regard to foreign juridical persons. Decree No. 49 of 13 January 1987 on the procedure for creating joint enterprises had excluded foreign citizens as potential founders of joint enterprises, providing that only foreign juridical persons could act in that capacity.[44]

---

[41]   SZ SSSR (1931) item 197; transl. in V. V. Gsovski, *Soviet Civil Law*, II, pp. 343-346.

[42]   Article 124, para. one. Transl. in W. E. Butler, *The Soviet Legal System: Legislation and Documentation* (1978) p. 427.

[43]   See M. I. Braginskii, W. E. Butler, and A. A. Rubanov (commentary), *The Law on Ownership in the USSR* (1991) pp.243-253.

[44]   Point 4. Although this Decree has been amended several times, point 4 remains unchanged as of Spring 1991

The Edict of the President of the USSR of 26 October 1990 on foreign investments took the next step, consolidating a new role for foreign citizens in the international turnover of the USSR by providing that foreign investors may be both foreign juridical persons and citizens.

The Edict determines three basic ways for foreign citizens to invest. First is the possibility of a participatory share in enterprises organised jointly with Soviet juridical persons, as well as with Soviet citizens. Next is the possibility of acquiring property, stocks, and other valuables. Third is the possible autonomous or joint acquisition jointly with Soviet juridical persons and Soviet citizens of the rights to use land and other property rights, including the acquisition of rights under a long-term lease in accordance with USSR and republic legislation. To these the 1991 FPForInv adds the creation of enterprises belonging wholly to the investors.

Enterprises with investments of foreign citizens may be created in any forms provided for by USSR and republic legislation.

As of August 1991, USSR and republic legislation had made provision for three forms of enterprise: joint-stock society, limited responsibility society, and the joint enterprise, any of which might qualify also as a small enterprise and thereby obtain certain tax and other privileges. Enabling legislation was awaited for various forms of partnership.

There are divergencies between Union and RSFSR legislation on joint-stock societies as regards the rights of foreign citizens. The USSR Statute on joint-stock societies and limited responsibility societies of 19 June 1990 provides that only Soviet citizens may be among natural persons who found a joint-stock society (point 38).[45] It further provides that "The peculiarities of participation of foreign ... citizens in joint-stock societies ... shall be determined by legislative acts of the USSR and the union and autonomous republics" (point 1). RSFSR legislation takes another position. The Statute on Joint-Stock Societies confirmed by the RSFSR Council of Ministers on 25 December 1990 provides: "foreign ... natural persons also may act in the role of founders in accordance with legislation on foreign investments" (point 11). It is provided that "societies with the participation of foreign ... natural persons shall be registered by the RSFSR Ministry of Finances in accordance with the present Statute and legislation of the RSFSR on foreign investments" (point 31).

As regards small enterprises, provision is made for them by the Decree of the USSR Council of Ministers of 8 August 1990. They include enterprises in industry and construction with up to 200 workers; science and scientific servicing, up to 100 persons; other branches of the production sphere, up to 50 persons; branches of the nonproduction sphere, up to 25 persons; and in retail trade, up to 15 persons.[46]

Foreign citizens may create enterprises on the territory of the USSR in which their investment amounts to 100% of the property. Such enterprises are juridical persons according to Soviet legislation.[47] According to this Edict, the profits of foreign citizens received in the USSR

---

[45]   Transl. in W. E. Butler (ed.), *Basic Documents on the Soviet Legal System* (2d ed., 1991), p. 331.

[46]   *SP SSSR* (1990), no. 19, item 101.

[47]   Article 2, Edict of President of USSR on Foreign Investments in the USSR. *Vedomosti SND SSSR* (1990) no. 44, item 944; transl. in M. I. Braginskii, W. E. Butler, and A. A. Rubanov (commentary), *The Law on Ownership in the USSR* (1991) pp. 311-313, reproduced as Annexe two herein.

in Soviet currency may be freely reinvested and used on the territory of the USSR in accordance with USSR and republic legislation and also transferred abroad in the procedure established by USSR legislation (point 4).

The provision of the FPInvA which recognised foreign citizens as subjects of investment activity and, consequently, investors is of special importance for the development of Soviet law despite the fact that it appeared after the Edict of 26 October 1990. Edicts of the President must be issued on the basis of and in execution of the USSR Constitution and laws of the USSR.[48] At the moment when the Edict of 26 October was enacted, neither the USSR Constitution nor all-union laws contained provisions recognising that foreign citizens had the right to be investors.

This provision of the FPInvA is the first provision of an all-union law to expressly recognise that role for foreign citizens in the Soviet economy, and has been reinforced by the 1991 FPForInv.

10. Neither the FPInvA nor preceding legislation contains special norms concerning the role of stateless persons in the sphere of investing. Nonetheless, the FPInvA indirectly resolves the issue of their status in this domain.

The FPInvA provides that Soviet citizens are subjects of investment activity, including as investors. The capacities granted to them to be investors are a step which determines the content of civil law capacity of Soviet citizens. The 1991 FPCivL provides that "... stateless persons shall enjoy in the USSR civil legal capacity on the

---

[48]   Article 127-5, introduced 14 March 1990 and amended 26 December 1990. *Vedomosti SND SSSR* (1991) no. 1, item 3.

same basis as Soviet citizens" (Article 160). By virtue of that provision, stateless persons are capable of being subjects of investment activity, including as investors.

11. The FPInvA names foreign States as being among potential investors. This provision is an innovation in Soviet law. It was never imagined that a foreign State might play such a role in Soviet economic life. Decree No. 49 of 13 January 1987 on joint enterprises never provided that a foreign State might be the founder of a joint enterprise. The 1990 USSR Law on Ownership contains a provision, to be sure, about the ownership of foreign States, but contemplates merely ownership necessary for that State to effectuate diplomatic, consular, and other international relations.[49]

Recognising that foreign States are capable of being investors is consistent with the general tenor of new political thinking and a departure from previous confrontationist positions.

However, Article 4 of the FPInvA is contradictory as regards the role of foreign States as subjects of investment activity. Point 1 provides that a foreign State may be either an investor or a "participant of investment activity." However, point 3 does not mention the foreign State amongst the "participants of investment activity."

12. The FPInvA does not name international inter-State organisations among potential investors. Stateless persons are in the same position, although with regard to them the principle of equalisation operates

---

[49]   Article 30. See M. I. Braginskii, W. E. Butler, and A. A. Rubanov (commentary), *The Law on Ownership in the USSR* (1991) pp. 279-280.

established by other laws (see Commentary to this Article, point 10 above). As regards international inter-State organisations, there are no rules in other laws equating them to any of the subjects named in the FPInvA. Such organisations are subjects of public international law, which also regulates their status. Municipal legislation may, of course, also contain rules governing them, but such rules are few in number. Neither the FPInvA nor other laws contained provisions enabling one to conclude that international inter-State organisations in the USSR are subjects of investment activity. This omission was finally repaired by the 1991 FPForInv, which expressly included "international organisations" and "stateless persons" as foreign investors.

The silence of the FPInvA on this issue is one of its greatest shortcomings. The consequences are so serious that it is difficult to imagine that the decision to omit international inter-State organisations was an oversight. There exist several large international inter-State organisations in the world which carry on extensive financial operations. Among them are the International Monetary Fund, the World Bank of Reconstruction and Development, and the European Bank for Reconstruction and Development. The Soviet Union has applied to join the first two and is a founding member of the last.

There is another important fact confirming the view that the silence of the FPInvA on this matter was deliberate. The FPInvA was adopted on 10 December 1990, that is, between the signature (29 May 1990) and ratification (26 March 1991) by the Soviet Union, of the Agreement Establishing The European Bank for Reconstruction and Development (EBRD), which is an international inter-State organisation of precisely this type.[50]

The founders of the EBRD are forty States, amongst them the United States, Japan, the Soviet Union, and sundry countries of Eastern and Western Europe. The capital fund of the EBRD is twelve billion dollars, of which the share of the Soviet Union is 600 million dollars. The principal task of the EBRD is to promote market reforms in Eastern Europe and the USSR. Pursuant to the Bank Charter, 60% of the EBRD loans are to be to the private sector and 40% to the State sector.

Against this background, the silence of the FPInvA concerning international inter-State organisations is astonishing. The FPInvA might have failed to draw attention to organisations of this type if the Soviet Union did not participate in such; but to turn one's back on those which the Soviet Union does join requires explanation.

The conclusion is unavoidable that the so-called "third path" of developing the Soviet economy reflected in the FPInvA (see point 2 of the Commentary to the Preamble) actually was directed towards improving the investment machinery which came into existence during the administrative-command era. The operations of a powerful investor orientated towards the private sector are completely alien to such machinery.

The FPInvA once again ignored its own raison d'etre set out in the Preamble: to promote the functioning of the national economy under conditions of the market economy. This position also creates other problems. But relations between the USSR and the EBRD are flourishing, and extensive cooperation with the Bank is developing in ways to promote the market economy in the Soviet Union. In particular, the EBRD is helping to finance the processes

[50] For the text of the Agreement, see I. F. I. Shihata, *The European Bank for Reconstruction and Development: A Comparative Analysis of the Constituent Agreement* (1990), pp. 109-152.

of destatisation and privatisation and to create a major private-sector investment bank to facilitate project financing. A branch of the EBRD is to be opened in Moscow, and Soviet business circles, both the State and non-State sectors, are giving evidence of a willingness to compete for EBRD loans.[51]

Soviet participation in the EBRD is but a first step towards full-scale participation in the International Monetary Fund and the World Bank.[52] The FPInvA is in the invidious position of having passed over in silence the key players in the processes of international investment cooperation.

13. Point 2, paragraph one, of this Article is yet another attempt by the FPInvA to work out a theoretical definition extemporaneously, not least because Soviet doctrinal writings have not considered the concept of an investor.

The definition of an investor as a subject taking a decision to invest valuables is satisfactory only with regard to the sphere of budget financing which is not to be repaid and which is effectuated within the framework of the administrative-command system. In that context it suffices to take the said decision in order to qualify as an investor. Under directive planning the recipient of an investment is obliged to accept the value and realise it, usually in the domain of capital construction. Consent to receive the investment is not required. The duty to receive it is laid down in the Plan.

---

[51]   *Kommersant*, no. 11 (1991), p. 10.

[52]   *Kommersant*, no. 13 (1991), p. 3.

During the transition to a market economy, this definition of an investor is too narrow. The FPInvA sees the investor through the prism of the administrative-command system. In a market economy a unilateral decision to invest valuables is inadequate as a decisive criterion for one to attain the status of an investor. It is essential that the recipient of the investor also have decided to receive the valuables to be invested. In the investment market the subject becomes an investment only when an agreement has been reached concerning the investment of the valuables between the subject and the recipient.

14. The distinction drawn between one's own, borrowed, and attracted valuables is connected with the classification of sources of financing investment activity set out in Article 9 of the FPInvA.

There is an inconsistency between this division and the definition of investment as all types of property and intellectual valuables (see Article 1). Such a distinction can be drawn only with regard to cash assets and is not applicable to other categories of valuables. For example, buildings, installations, and equipment can be neither borrowed nor attracted. The same is true of property rights arising from copyright. And one can hardly separate the right to use land and other natural resources into one's own, borrowed, and attracted categories.

15. The rule contained in point 2, paragraph two, of this Article seeks to explain and clarify the definition of investor given in paragraph one of this same point. The FPInvA clarifies that the investor may act in three roles:

depositor, creditor, and purchaser. However, the first of these has already been said in the very definition of an investor as a subject who takes a decision to invest.

The juxtaposition of the roles of creditor and purchaser is legally incorrect. In civil law the concept of an investor is a broad one. There is a creditor in all contracts, including purchase-sale contracts; there the purchaser is a creditor demanding the transfer of a thing. Therefore when the FPInvA provides that an investor may act as a creditor, it simultaneously resolves positively the question of whether the investor may act as a purchaser.

The provision of the FPInvA that an investor may fulfil the functions of any participant of investment activity is hardly successful either. A participant of investment activity is a subject ensuring the effectuation of investment on the basis of orders or commissions (see Commentary to Article 4[3]). Apparently the language is intended to mean that a subject, being an investor, has the right simultaneously to perform the commissions of other investors. Evidently the FPInvA is attempting to react to situations when in some relations the same subject acts as an investor and in others as the executor of someone's commissions. It is doubtful whether the FPInvA should have pursued this matter. There are some things which are self-evident.

16. The definition of a "participant of investment activity" in point 3 of this Article is noteworthy especially because it does not encompass the recipient of an investment. The FPInvA views the domain of investment through the prism of the administrative-command system and the budget financing peculiar to that system based on directive planning. Consequently, the FPInvA having defined a recipient as the "object of entrepreneurial (or other) activity" (see the Commentary to Article 1), one

might have expected some legal clarification (see Commentary to Article 2[2]).

It follows from the definition given that the recipient of investments is not considered to be a participant of investment activity. The recipient is thus outside the sphere of regulation of the FPInvA and all legislation on investment activity.

This further demonstrates the anti-market nature of the FPInvA. Having in Article 1 described the investment market as the juxtaposition of valuables and objects of entrepreneurial activity, the FPInvA then changed its perception and began to regard investment activity not as a sphere in which there must be competition amongst investors and recipients of investments for the most advantageous terms for granting and receiving investments, but rather as a domain in which the recipients of investments do not figure at all.

The FPInvA consequently views investment activity as a domain where relations are formed between investors who are treated as subjects accepting unilateral decisions to invest valuables (see Commentary to Article 4[2]) and as subjects who ensure the effectuation of those decisions on the basis of orders or commissions. This typical investor originates conceptually within the administrative-command system.

17. The FPInvA recognises as a participant of investment activity subjects who operate as the executors of orders or on the basis of a commission of an investor.

Behind this somewhat abstract formulation there is concealed the principal investor who invests within the framework of the administrative-command system on the basis of budget investing. These are specialised State organisations of the construction industry. There are many such organisations, some of enormous size with tens of thousands of workers, engineers, and employees. Amongst them are specialised construction organisations, assembly organisations, and design organisations and institutes. It is they who are at the centre of attention of the FPInvA.

In their midst within recent years there have appeared construction cooperatives, some of which are highly efficient. And the Decree of the USSR Council of Ministers of 8 August 1990 on the creation of small enterprises made it possible for citizens, family members, and other persons who jointly conduct a labour economy to create small enterprises in the field of construction with up to 200 workers.[53]

The provisions of the FPInvA to the effect that a participant of investment activity operates as the executor of an order are a reference back to the legal norms which regulate the relations of a customer with his contracting parties. These are principally the norms of civil law concerning the independent-work contract in capital construction. Civil legislation calls one of the parties to such a contract the customer, and the other, the independent-work contractor.

The 1961 FPCivL provided that by an "independent work contract for capital construction, an independent contractor-organisation shall be obliged to build with its own efforts and means and to surrender to the customer-organisation an object provided for by the plan in accordance with confirmed design estimate documentation and within the established period, and the customer shall be obliged to grant to the independent contractor a building site, to transfer the confirmed design estimate documentation to him, to ensure the timely

---

[53]   *SP SSSR* (1990), no. 19, item 101.

financing of the construction, to accept the objects whose construction is completed, and to pay for them."[54]

As regards the structure of capital construction contracts, the 1961 FPCivL provided that an independent work contract for capital construction is concluded by a customer with one construction organisation and, in the instances and procedure determined by the USSR Council of Ministers, with two or more construction organisations, which have the right as the general independent work contractor to entrust the fulfilment of individual units of work to specialised organisations on the basis of a sub-independent work contract. The contract for the fulfilment of work for the assembly of equipment is concluded with the customer or with the general independent work contractor or with the supplier of the equipment. Contracts for the fulfilment of assembly and other special work may, with the consent of the general independent work contractor, be concluded by a customer with assembly or other specialised organisations.

The customer effectuates control and technical supervision over the conformity of the amount, cost, and quality of work fulfilled to the designs and estimates. He has the right at any time to verify the course and the quality of construction and assembly work, and also the quality of materials used, without interfering in the operational and economic activity of the independent work contractor (Articles 68 and 69).

As from 1 January 1992 the 1991 FPCivL enter into force. It contains a new definition of the independent work contract for capital construction which eliminates references to organisations, plan, estimates, and other

---

[54]   Article 67. Translated in W. E. Butler (comp. & transl.), *The Soviet Legal System: Selected Contemporary Legislation and Documentation* (1978), p. 413

terms characteristic of the administrative-command period.[55]

The FPInvA reference to the executors of orders also has in view the norms concerning an independent work contract for the performance of design and survey work. Such contracts were prior to 1992 governed by subordinate Soviet legislation, but have been expressly included in the 1991 FPCivL. Under such contracts one of the parties likewise is called the customer. The independent work contractor is obliged to work out design documentation pursuant to the planning task of the customer and to fulfil survey work, and the customer is obliged to accept the work and pay for it. The independent work contractor bears responsibility for design defects except for those elicited after the periods provided by the contract elapse. When defects are discovered, the independent work contractor is obliged to redo the design without compensation and compensate the customer for losses caused by the design defects unless the contract or legislation otherwise provide (Article 96).

Finally, the FPInvA reference to executors of orders also has in view the norms regulating a contract for the fulfilment of scientific research or experimental construction design work. This contract too is expressly regulated in the 1991 FPCivL (Article 97). The executor is obliged to perform scientific research stipulated by the planning task, work out a model of a new manufacture or construction designs for it, of new production technology or other production innovation, and the customer is obliged to accept the work and pay for it.

---

[55]   Chapter 12, especially Article 95. See W. E. Butler (intro. & transl.), *The USSR Fundamental Principles of Civil Legislation* (1991).

18. The provision of the FPInvA that participants of investment activity are subjects "ensuring the effectuation of investments" is formulated broadly and will facilitate the transition to the market. Such participants would include broker firms operating in the stock exchange.

Stock exchange institutions existed in the Soviet Union from 1922 and performed stock exchange operations. They were abolished by a Decree of the Central Executive Committee and the USSR Council of People's Commissars on 6 February 1930.

From late 1990 early steps have been taken in the Soviet Union to re-create the stock exchanges. Two types of such institutions have been created: autonomous stock exchanges and stock exchange sections within goods exchanges. Stock exchanges now exist in several cities of the Soviet Union,[56] and broker firms have been established. Amongst the latter is a firm called "Russian Securities," whose charter provides for offering financial brokering,[57] and such firms as "Moscow Securities," "Brokinvest-servis," and "Russian Brokerage House S. A. and Ko."[58]

The FPInvA provides that the participants of investment activity operate as the executor of orders or on the basis of the commission of an investor. This merely defines in the most general legal form the legal aspect of relations of broker firms with clients. There are no special norms as yet in Soviet civil legislation regulating stock exchange transactions. However, the general norms concerning contracts are relevant, as are those regulating

---

[56]   On the Protocols concerning the founding of the Moscow Stock Exchange, see *Pravitel' stvennyi vestnik*, no. 48 (1990) p. 2.

[57]   *Izvestiia*, 24 January 1991, p. 4.

[58]   *Kommersant*, no. 13 (1991), p. 24.

contracts of guarantee, commission agency, and representation.

Detailed rules governing stock exchange transactions may be expected in the imminent future.

19. Among the participants of investment activity the FPInvA names foreign juridical persons and foreign citizens. In practice many foreign juridical persons are conducting economic operations in the Soviet Union on the basis of independent work contracts for capital construction.

Soviet law deems an independent work contract for capital construction concluded between a Soviet party and a foreign party to be a foreign economic transaction under the 1991 FPCivL. The form of a foreign economic transaction concluded by Soviet juridical persons and citizens, irrespective of the place where such transactions are concluded, is determined by legislation of the USSR (Article 165).[59] The 1991 FPCivL further provides that the form of transactions with regard to structures and other immovable property in the USSR are subordinate to Soviet law. The independent work contract for capital construction effectuated in the USSR usually affects such property.

The rights and duties of the parties regarding foreign economic transactions are determined according to the law of the country chosen by the parties when concluding the transaction or by virtue of a later agreement. If the parties have not chosen applicable law then the law of the country where such activity is effectuated or where the results provided for by the contracts concerning the fullfilment of

---

[59]   See W. E. Butler (intro. & transl.), *The USSR Fundamental Principles of Civil Legislation* (1991).

construction, assembly, and other works relating to capital construction (Article 166[2]).

20. The provision of the FPInvA concerning executors of orders and commissions also creates a legal basis for foreign juridical or natural persons acting as brokers in Soviet stock exchanges. But further legislation will be required to determine the conditions of access and the status of foreigners in this domain.

Soviet exchanges are offering seats to foreign juridical persons payable in hard currency.

Article 5: Legislation of USSR and Union and Autonomous Republics on Investment Activity

Relations connected with the effectuation of investment activity in the USSR shall be regulated by the present Fundamental Principles and by legislative acts of the USSR and the union and autonomous republics issued in accordance therewith.

Investment activity shall be regulated:

of Soviet subjects abroad, by legislation of the country on whose territory this activity is effectuated, by respective international treaties, as well as by special legislation of the USSR and union republics;

of foreign subjects in the USSR, as well as of Soviet and foreign subjects in free economic zones in the USSR, by the present Fundamental Principles and by special legislation of the USSR and union and autonomous republics.

1. The provisions of Article 5, paragraph one, appertain to that type of norm which is found in all laws of the USSR categorised as "Fundamental Principles of Legislation of the USSR and Union Republics." These laws are established, as a rule, for a particular branch of law and include only basic norms, leaving the resolution of the remaining issues to other legislative acts, most notably those of the union republics.

The legal basis of this scheme is the 1977 USSR Constitution, which confers on the Union the right to establish fundamental principles of legislation of the USSR and union republics (Article 73[4])[60] It contains no limitations with respect to the domain in which laws of this type may be introduced.

The political crisis that developed between the Union and the republics in 1989-91 has had a number of legal consequences. Among them, the issue has been raised as to the right of the Union to issue laws of this type. The July 1991 draft Treaty of the Union proposed that the USSR would have the right to establish fundamental principles of legislation only with regard to questions agreed with the republics (Article 5) [61] If this provision is retained in the final redaction, the FPInvA will turn out to be a law adopted before the conclusion of the Treaty but without the consent of the republics.

It is possible, of course, that the republics will give the subsequent consent. It should be borne in mind though that in 1990 all the republics proclaimed their State sovereignty, and some -- notably the Russian Federation and the Ukraine -- proclaimed the principle of the supremacy of their laws over laws of the USSR. With the enactment of the FPInvA the USSR in essence proposed to the republics that they seriously restructure their own legislation and adopt acts effectuating the aggregate regulation of all questions connected with investment activity.

What the outcome will be can not be predicted. Were it to be favourable, the republic legislation on investment activity would be based on the FPInvA and the structure of the legislation would not differ from the usual structure in other domains. But were the republics to take a negative

---

[60]   Translated in W. E. Butler (ed.), *Basic Documents on the Soviet Legal System* (2d ed., 1991), p. 17.

[61]   *Izvestiia*, 9 March 1991, p. 2, cols. 1-5.

attitude towards this approach, the FPInvA would become uniquely a foundation on which nothing was built. Only certain other legislative acts of the USSR would rest, at best, on its provisions.

2. The provisions of paragraph two of this Article have no parallel in Soviet legislation. They represent information about the legal milieu in which investment activity is to be effectuated, but incorporated in the text of a law and set out in the form of a legal norm. The two provisions which comprise paragraph two only appear to be legal norms at first glance. But in fact they are not rules of behaviour regulating relations, but a notification of the legislator directed to the participants of investment activity. Taken as a whole, paragraph two is a literary work setting out certain information about legal phenomena.

The FPInvA gives the information separately for Soviet and foreign subjects. The principal concern is to explain the situation to Soviet participants of investment activity performed abroad. The law informs Soviet juridical persons that when effectuating investment operations outside the Soviet Union they shall be concerned both with legislation of the respective foreign State and legislation of the USSR and republics. The FPInvA cautions them that in undertaking investment operations abroad they must, on one hand, be aware that they are in the sphere of the operation of foreign law and can not rely only on Soviet law as they are accustomed to in their ordinary activities. On the other hand, the FPInvA warns them not to be deluded that when operating abroad they fall entirely outside the effects of Soviet legislation.

The FPInvA having been adopted on 10 December 1990, the context of Soviet legislative development must be borne in mind. Before 1 April 1989 all foreign economic operations in the USSR were effectuated by a limited number of specialised State organisations, mostly foreign trade associations. The Decree of the USSR Council of Ministers of 2 December 1988 on the further development of foreign economic activity of State, cooperative, and other social enterprises, associations, and organisations endowed all enterprises, associations, production cooperatives, and other organisations with the right to directly effectuate export-import operations.[62]

More than 30,000 Soviet juridical and natural persons have taken advantage of this right and begun to carry out foreign trade operations. In the course of this, for them, new activity they have increasingly encountered opportunities for investment operations. However, the Decree of 2 December 1988 merely mentioned operations relating to export and import. Investing abroad, as before, was engaged in by a tiny number of specialised State organisations.

On 18 May 1989 the USSR Council of Ministers adopted a decree on the development of the economic activity of Soviet organisations abroad which provided that such activity must be performed by creating enterprises with abroad Soviet participation in their capital, by investing in the revenue assets or securities of other enterprises, and by operations in the commodity and stock exchanges. It was established that Soviet State enterprises, associations, and organisations, as well as consortiums organised with their participation, joint-stock societies, trade houses, and associations might create foreign enterprises and engage in operations with securities (Article 3).[63]

---

[62]   *SP SSSR* (1989), no. 2, item 7

[63]   *SP SSSR* (1989) no. 24, item 82; transl. in W. E. Butler (ed.), *Basic Documents on*

The Decree regulated relations which are formed within the Soviet Union in connection with the creation of foreign enterprises by introducing an authorisation procedure. It was established that foreign enterprises are created by Soviet State enterprises, associations, and organisations with the consent of superior ministries or departments of the USSR or the union republic councils of ministers, taking into account the recommendations of the USSR Ministry of Foreign Economic Relations and the USSR Ministry of Foreign Affairs. Joint-stock societies, associations, trade houses, consortiums, as well as State enterprises, associations, and organisations which are not within the system of ministries or departments create foreign enterprises with the consent of the USSR Ministry of Foreign Economic Relations and taking into account the recommendations of the USSR Ministry of Foreign Affairs. Production cooperatives, unions thereof, and other social organisations may also create them in the same procedure.

It was established that foreign enterprises are registered by Soviet partners in the register kept by the USSR Ministry of Finances.

The operations of Soviet partners with securities are performed either through the Vneshekonombank SSSR or Soviet banks abroad, or independently, but with subsequent information concerning the operations to be supplied to the USSR Ministry of Finances and USSR Ministry of Foreign Economic Relations.

When the FPInvA was enacted, numerous legal questions were being raised about the new opportunities being opened. Soviet juridical persons, usually with enormous difficulty, were more or less orientating

the Soviet Legal System (2d ed., 1991) pp. 489-492

themselves in the complexities of export and import operations, but in the domain of investment they felt completely lost. This provision of the FPInvA was an attempt to respond to the problem.

But whatever the benign intentions of the legislator, paragraph two went beyond the limits of the law. A literary work has no place in a piece of legislation, and the formulation is, moreover, rather controversial.

3. The provision of the FPInvA addressed to the Soviet participant in investment activity is not a conflicts norm, although it has been composed in a form which recalls the form usually used by conflicts rules. A conflicts norm indicates which of several possible laws regulate a relation. The FPInvA does not make a choice of law; it merely names both foreign and Soviet legislation, together with international treaties (see point 5 of the Commentary below).

Since the provision here considered is not a conflicts rule, the FPInvA makes no changes whatever in the private international law of the USSR. Transactions concluded by Soviet juridical persons with foreign contracting parties when effectuating investments directed from the Soviet Union abroad are foreign trade transactions. They are regulated by conflicts norms contained in the 1991 FPCivL, which stipulate that "The form of foreign trade transactions performed by Soviet juridical persons and citizens, irrespective of the place of performance of those transactions, shall be determined by legislation of the USSR" (Article 165, paragraph two) [64] The form of a transaction between a Soviet investor and foreign recipient

---

[64]   See W. E. Butler (intro. & transl.), *The USSR Fundamental Principles of Civil Legislation* (1991).

which governs the movement of valuables being invested from the USSR abroad will not be regulated by legislation of the foreign State on whose territory the investment activity is being effectuated. It will always be determined by Soviet law.

This provision of the FPInvA in no way alters the issue of the choice of law regulating foreign trade transactions. The 1991 FPCivL provides that the rights and duties of the parties with regard to a transaction are determined by the law of the place where it is performed unless otherwise established by agreement of the parties (Article 165), and as regards a foreign trade contract, the rights and duties of the parties are determined according to the law of the country selected by the parties when concluding the contract or by virtue of subsequent agreement (Article 166). Therefore the rights and duties of parties to a contract concluded by a Soviet investor and a foreign partner and governing the movement of valuables being invested from the USSR abroad will be determined by the law of the country on whose territory the investment activity is being effectuated, as a rule, if the parties chose that law.

In the absence of such a choice, the law of the country on whose territory the investment activity is being effetuated will apply if the conflicts norms of the 1991 FPCivL so prescribe. There are such norms. For example, the law of the country where a joint enterprise is estaglished with the participation of foreign juridicial persons and citizens is applicable to the contract creating it (Article 166[3]). And there are other conflicts norms which under certain conditions may lead to a similar result. But there is no general conflicts norm in Soviet law referring to the law of the country on whose territory investment activity is effectuated.

4.   The second provision in Article 5, paragraph two, also is addressed to foreign subjects of investment activity and likewise is not a norm of law but rather a literary product. Unlike the provisions intended for Soviet subjects, it is a literary overindulgence, since foreign juridical and natural persons live in a world where the international capital markets are functioning. It is not necessary to explain to them that when making an investment in the Soviet Union they should bear in mind that they are entering the domain of Soviet law. The explanation nonetheless is given, probably for the pedantic reason that if something is explained to Soviet subjects, the same should be said to foreign subjects.

Since this provision of the FPInvA was not a legal rule but a work of literature, it exerts no influence on the legal status of foreign juridical and natural persons in the USSR. The words of the FPInvA that investment activity of foreign subjects in the USSR is regulated by the FPInvA itself and by special legislation does not mean that such activity is thereby removed from the operation of general norms of Soviet law. General Soviet civil legislation, legislation on ownership, and other enactments also apply to it.

5.   The FPInvA does not contain rules affecting international treaties. The Soviet theory of international law proceeds from the fact that international law and municipal law are two autonomous systems of law which closely interact in a complex way. In various Soviet laws there are numerous rules which speak of international law and of international treaties. Such provisions are to be found also in legislation regulating relations connected with investment activity. The 1991 FPCivL provides that "If other rules have been established by an international

treaty in which the USSR participates than those which are contained in Soviet civil legislation, the rules of the international treaty shall apply" (Article 170) [65]

The Soviet Union has concluded more than a dozen international treaties containing provisions relating to investments. Some are of a general character. For example, the Treaty on Amity and Cooperation between the USSR and France of 29 October 1990 provides that the parties will endeavour to improve the conditions of activity of enterprises of the country of the partner in the domain of direct investments and protection of invested capital (Article 16). Other international treaties are devoted specially to investment. Among them is the Soviet-Finnish Agreement on Promoting the Effectuation and Mutual Protection of Capital Investments of 8 February 1989. It provides, in particular, that none of the parties will take coercive measures relating to the seizure of capital investments effectuated by investors of the other Party. On 29 May 1991 the USSR Supreme Soviet ratified fourteen bilateral investment protection treaties, including that with the United Kingdom which entered into force on 3 July 1991.

Article 5, paragraph two, of the FPInvA does not contain legal norms resolving questions of the interaction of Soviet law with international law. As already noted, the formulation is purely a work of literature, and the reference to international treaties has no legal consequences.

Further, an error of considerable importance must be noted. The FPInvA informs Soviet participants in investment activity that when effectuating operations abroad they should have respective international treaties in

---

[65]   See W. E. Butler (intro. & transl.), *USSR Fundamental Principles of Civil Legislation* (1991).

view. However, the FPInvA is silent about international treaties when addressing foreign subjects of investment activity in the USSR. There is no basis for doing so. All treaties concluded by the USSR and affecting investments are of a bilateral character. In practice the treaty provisions are more important for foreign investors in the USSR than they are for Soviet investors in the respective foreign States.

We stress that it does not follow from the FPInvA provisions considered here that Soviet law attaches force only to those provisions of international treaties concluded by the USSR which are useful for Soviet juridical persons operating abroad and overlooks those directed towards protecting foreign juridical and natural persons in the USSR. The Soviet Union accepts the generally-recognised principle of international law concerning the good-faith and complete fulfilment by States of their obligations under international law. This principle is reflected in the USSR Constitution.

Section II: Effectuation of Investment Activity

Article 6: Rights of Investors

1. All investors shall have equal rights with regard to the effectuation of investment activity.

The use by an investor of property and intellectual valuables for investment in objects not prohibited by the present Fundamental Principles and other legislation of the USSR and the union and autonomous republics shall be recognised, without any limitations whatever, to be his inherent right and shall be protected by law.

2. An investor shall autonomously determine the amount, orientations, and effectiveness of investments effectuated and shall at his discretion attract on a contractual basis citizens and juridical persons needed to realise the investments.

3. By decision of the investor the rights of possession, use, and disposition of investments and the results of their effectuation may be transferred to other citizens and juridical persons in the procedure established by law. Mutual relations of the parties under the said transfer of rights shall be regulated on the basis of contracts.

4. Financial assets may be attracted for investing in the form of credits and the issuance in the procedure established by legislation of securities and loans.

The property of an investor may be used by him to secure his obligations. Only that property which belongs to the borrower by right of ownership or by right of full economic jurisdiction, unless provided otherwise by legislative acts of the USSR and the union and autonomous republics, may be accepted on pledge. Pledged property may, in the event pledge obligations are violated, be realised in the procedure established by legislation.

5.   An investor shall have the right to possess, use, and dispose of objects and the results of investments, including reinvestment and trade operations on the territory of the USSR, in accordance with legislative acts of the USSR and the union and autonomous republics.

Objects, investment in which shall not entail the acquisition of the rights of ownership to them, may be determined by legislation of the USSR and the union and autonomous republics, which shall not exclude the possibility of subsequent possession, operative management, or participation of the investor in the revenues from the operation of such objects.

6.   An investor shall have the right to acquire the property needed by him from citizens and juridical persons directly or through intermediaries at prices and on conditions determined by arrangement of the parties, unless this is contrary to legislation, without limitation in amount or nomenclature.

1. This Section of the FPInvA places the investor at the very centre of regulation. The second type of subjects of investment activity -- the participant of investment activity -- here is a secondary consideration. This Article, separate and detailed, is devoted to investors, whereas as participants of investment activity have no separate Article devoted to them.

There are no norms in this Section of the FPInvA devoted to the recipients of investments. The general view of the FPInvA is to ignore their existence. Notwithstanding this silence, it is evident that the recipients of investments are immediately behind the scenes: the norms defining the rights of investors affect the interests of the recipients of investments.

2. The rules in point 1 of this Article will play an important role if the Soviet Union continues to move towards the market economy. Articles 1 and 2 of the FPInvA provide for a plurality of investors. But at present the investors are in an unequal position: the State is the principal investor. In the future investment market there must be competition amongst investors. The rule concerning the equal rights of investors may become a sound legal base for investment.

The FPInvA provides that "all investors" have equal rights. This means that no type of investor may be deprived of any rights connected with the effectuation of investment activity. The principle of being endowed with equal rights also appertains to foreign juridical persons, foreign citizens, and foreign States when they act as investors.

3. The FPInvA has used the category of "inherent right" to characterise the legal status of the investor. The FPInvA is undertaking with this formulation to achieve the maximum possible degree of legal security for the legal status of the investor. As the Soviet Union moves towards the market economy, this concept may play a positive role.

It is appropriate to note that the concept of inherent right has not been used at all in earlier Soviet legislation. The FPInvA is the first all-union law to use this category in this sense. Its appearance is a consequence of the influence of international law on Soviet law. The concept appears in the International Covenant on Civil and Political Rights, which provides that "Every human being has the inherent right to life. This right shall be protected by law" (Article 6[1])[66]

The effort of the FPInvA to create a very stable legal base for the investor is consistent with the tasks which arise in connection with the transition to the market economy. Perhaps the phrase "inherent right" is even a bit too strong. The International Covenant on Civil and Political Rights used the expression only once, and then in connection with the most important human right. Ultimately, whether to invest or not is not a Shakesperean question: "to be or not to be."

Three conclusions follow from the right of the investor proclaimed by the FPInvA to be an inherent right. First, this right juridically speaking is placed higher than the law (lex) itself. No law, including laws of a constitutional stature, may deprive an investor of the right to use all types of property and intellectual valuables for investing. Further, an investor may not be deprived of this

---

[66]   See the text of the Covenant in *International Legal Materials*, VI (1967), 370.

inalienable right by the issuance of any subordinate act or act of an agency of administration.

It follows, moreover, that the investor himself may not voluntarily renounce or waive his inherent right or limit that right. A contract concluded by him which contained a provision renouncing, waiving, or limiting this right would be void as contrary to Article 6(1) of the FPInvA.

The final conclusion relates to the effectuation of this inherent right by an investor. The FPInvA provides that no limitations whatever are permitted with respect to the use by an investor of valuables for investing. The possibility of legal rules being created which would introduce limitations on the investor effectuating his right is thereby excluded. We refer here to the establishment, for example, of an authorisation procedure, or requirements for some sort of registration, or the introduction of conditions which would impede investing. The provision on the inadmissibility of limitations also prohibits agencies of administration from performing acts which would create obstacles against specific investors.

4.   Point 1 of this Article contains a serious gap. Having satisfactorily resolved the issue of the rights of investors, it is silent about the duties of investors. The legal status of subjects is determined not only by the rights which they have, but also by the duties they must perform.

Generally speaking, the FPInvA does refer to duties: Article 8 is entitled "Duties of Subjects of Investment Activity." But the FPInvA does not proclaim the principle of the equality of the duties of investors. From the standpoint of the transition to the market economy, this would have been of considerable importance. All investors in the market must be equal from the standpoint of duties imposed on them. However, equality of rights is not sufficient in itself to ensure equal fundamental legal conditions for competition. It could happen that although having equal rights some subjects of investment activity have additional duties which affects their performance in the market.

The development of Soviet law shows that the absence of this principle could lead to the destruction of market relations. In the late 1920s the method of worsening the position of private entrepreneurs was extensively used by imposing the duty on them to pay taxes which were not merely discriminatory but sufficiently onerous to remove those entrepreneurs from trade and production.

5.   The FPInvA provides that the effectuation by an investor of his inherent right is limited. There are objects in which investment is prohibited by the FPInvA itself or by other Union and republic legislation (see Commentary to Article 3).

Here there is a parallel with the International Covenant on Civil and Political Rights, for having proclaimed the right to life to be an inherent human right, the Covenant nonetheless allows capital punishment (Article 6[2]).

6.   Although point 2 of this Article has the form of a norm of law, in truth it is a literary passage which explains to an investor what his legal possibilities are. The explanation is set out in a form which presupposes a juridically illiterate audience.

Even as a literary exercise the provision deserves comment. The clause reads that the investor "attracts citizens and juridical persons," presumably at his discretion. The concept of attracting is a unilateral act of an agency of power. An analogous formulation is used in the FPCrimP with respect to an accused person (Article 4).[67]

The FPInvA provides that the "attraction" of investment is to occur on a contractual basis. This is impossible. An investor may only offer to conclude a contract with citizens and juridical persons, but not to attract them at his discretion.

The FPInvA also is ambiguous in providing that an investor autonomously determines the amounts and orientations of the investments being effectuated. This is true only with respect to budget investing not subject to repayment undertaken by way of directive planning. In the investment market an investor will not have the right to decide these issues unilaterally. The recipient of the investment also will have a choice, which the FPInvA omitted to mention both here and elsewhere (see Commentary to Article 4[3]).

Finally, the FPInvA is careless in stipulating that the effectiveness of investments is determined by the investor, that is, presumably at his discretion. Perhaps the legislator wished to say that the investor has the right to evaluate their future effectiveness. But the word "determine" has been used. In reality effectiveness will be determined by objective economic circumstances.

---

[67]   The reference is to the 1958 Fundamental Principles of Criminal Procedure of the USSR and Union Republics, transl. in W. E. Butler, *Collected Legislation of the USSR and Constituent Union Republics* (1979-). Analogous language appears in Article 4(1) of the 1991 Fundamental Principles of Criminal Procedure Legislation of the USSR and Republics. See *Izvestiia*, 28 June 1991, pp. 4-5.

7. Point 3 of this Article is a consequence of the provision of the FPInvA in Article 6(5), which endows an investor with the right of ownership in the object of investment, as well as the right of possession, use, and disposition of the results of the investment. Since the investor has been placed in this legal position by Article 6(5), here the FPInvA gives to the investor the right to decide to transfer the rights in an investment to third persons as well as the results of the effectuation thereof. We stress that the FPInvA does not require the consent of the recipient of the investment. A contract must be concluded between the investor and the person to whom the investment rights are being transferred.

This provision also follows from the failure of the FPInvA to address the status of recipients of investments. Here this omission is so far-reaching that the norm in aggregate with those contained in Article 6(5) leads to the recipients of investments being expelled from the investment market, thereby preventing an investment market from being created in the Soviet Union.

8. The FPInvA in general suffers from repetitions (see Commentary to the Preamble). Repeated most frequently are attempts to classify the sources for financing investment activity. Article 4(2) already has provided that investors may use their own, borrowed, or attracted valuables. And the FPInvA also contains Article 9 on the sources of financing investment activity, which basically reiterates the same classification (see Commentary to Article 9).

Nonetheless, paragraph one of point 4 of this Article returns to the question. The list is hardly successful. Loans and credits are one and the same thing. The issuance of securities is inaccurately depicted as a type of financial assets. The issuance of securities is a business operation. Financial assets are those assets received from such issuance.

9.   Paragraph two of Article 6(4) is devoted to a very important issue: the right of pledge. In the 1920s Soviet civil codes contained norms concerning the right of pledge which corresponded to market relations existing at that time in the Soviet Union and were of an acceptable legal standard. During the period of the administrative-command system, the right of pledge was at best of a rudimentary nature. The 1961 FPCivL provided that "enterprises, buildings, installations, equipment, and other property relegated to the basic assets of a State organisation may not be the subject of a pledge ..."[68]

As a result, the norms concerning the right of pledge contained in the union republic civil codes came to be applied to obligations with the participation of citizens. In practice the pledge of structures which belonged to citizens were pledged under a bank credit, or things were pledged in a pawnshop. Further, the pledge of property in turnover was provided for in rules issued by the State Bank of the USSR and was used in the carriage of freight by rail. But in practice the levying of execution against pledged property virtually never occurred.

10. The turning point came with the adoption of the 1990 USSR Law on Ownership, which provided that "execution may be levied with regard to the obligations of

---

[68]   Article 22. Transl. in W. E. Butler (comp. & transl.), *The Soviet Legal System: Legislation and Documentation* (1978), p. 400. Article 23 of the same enactment provided that execution could not be levied against property relegated to the basic assets of collective farms or other cooperative organisations with regard to claims of creditors. *Ibid*, p. 401

a juridical person against any property belonging to it by right of ownership or full economic jurisdiction, as well as operative management ..."[69] This Law opened the door for the creation of norms on the right of pledge what would be adequate to an economy in transition to a market economy.

The FPInvA is the first law which made a step in this direction. But this step was less than modest and not entirely satisfactory.

11. The positive element in this provision is the indication that the property of an investor might be used in order to ensure his obligations. No exceptions were made for investors who hold State ownership. Things in State ownership thus in principle may be the object of a pledge. This conclusion flows from the aforecited rules in the 1990 USSR Law on Ownership.

However, the FPInvA has not resolved all of the issues which arise in connection with the pledge of things which are State ownership. They provided in general form that the object of a pledge must be either in the ownership of the borrower or must belong to the borrower by right of full economic jurisdiction.

The application of this norm to the pledge of things which are in State ownership creates a rather peculiar situation. In the sphere of State ownership, any property belonging to someone by right of full economic jurisdiction simultaneously belongs to another subject by right of ownership. The FPInvA has thus created a situation where there are two subjects which have the right to pledge the same thing in order to secure their own respective obligation.

---

[69]   Article 5(1). See M. I. Braginskii, W. E. Butler, and A. A. Rubanov (commentary), *The Law on Ownership in the USSR* (1991), pp. 69-75.

The 1990 USSR Law on Ownership provides that "property which is in State ownership and has been allocated to a State enterprise shall belong to it by right of full economic jurisdiction."[70] This same Law relegates to State ownership the all-union ownership, the ownership of union republics, the ownership of autonomous republics, autonomous regions, autonomous national areas, and other administrative-territorial formations. The soviet of people's deputies effectuates the disposition and administration of State property, together with agencies which it duly empowers to do so (Article 19[1]). Disposition for these purposes would include the right of pledge.

The provision whereby two subjects which have things in State ownership may pledge them makes matters rather difficult, especially for bank credits.

12. Point 5 of this Article at first glance is directed towards protecting the interests of investors in the future investment market. The FPInvA gives to investors the right of ownership in the object in which the investment is made and the right of possession, use, and disposition of the results of the investment. Further, the FPInvA provides that when legislation specifies those instances when an investor does not receive the right of ownership in an object of investment, the investor must be given the right to later take the object into his possession. Moreover, Article 6(3) provides that by decision of the investor the right of possession, use, and disposition of investments and the results of their effectuation may be transferred by the investor to other citizens and juridical persons (see Commentary to Article 6[3]).

---

[70]   Article 24(1). See M. I. Braginskii, W. E. Butler, and A. A. Rubanov (commentary), *The Law on Ownership in the USSR* (1991) pp. 225-231.

The concern of the FPInvA for the interests of the investor in and of itself is consistent with the tasks confronting Soviet law during the transition to the market economy. Law must protect he who risks most in the market. It is the investor beyond doubt who does so since the valuables invested belong to him.

Everything must have reasonable limits, however. Points 3 and 5 of this Article transcend those limits, for the recipient of investments lacks such legal protection. Under the legal regulation established by the FPInvA, the consent of the recipient to receive investments automatically entails for him the loss of the right of ownership in the object of entrepreneurial activity and his being cut off from the results of the investing. The situation in which the FPInvA places the recipient of investments will not facilitate the transition to the market economy. Under these conditions the recipients in the future market will regret even more the procedures which existed under the administrative-command system. The FPInvA has created legal conditions for recipients which cannot be sustained in the future investment market, and thus has undermined the very idea of the market. Only superficially does the FPInvA seem to be concerned about the interests of investors. In substance the FPInvA creates legal conditions which simply make it impossible for investors to offer to invest their property and intellectual valuables.

13. Point 5 of this Article creates serious problems for the entirety of Soviet law, especially civil law. The FPInvA undertakes to create a special system of legal norms regulating relations which are connected with operations relating to investment. These are principles not expressed as specialised rules isolated in an autonomous branch of law, but rather an attempt to create norms based

on completely different principles than those of the civil law.

The FPInvA in Article 1 describes the investment market as the juxtaposition of two aspects: investments (that is, all property and intellectual valuables) and objects of entrepreneurial activity. The term "investment" is used to describe the links existing between these two aspects. The FPInvA takes the view that there is some sort of immutable link between the investor and the object of investment, and indeed the concept of investment is treated extremely broadly as a category expressing the link of any objects of entrepreneurial activity with the possessors of all types of property and intellectual valuables. It encompasses the most diverse types of economic relations and, most importantly, the most diverse types of legal relations (see Commentary to Article 1).

This point of the FPInvA provides that only one civil-law consequence arises from all permissible types of "investment," namely, that the investor acquires the right of ownership in the object of investment. The investor's right of ownership is expressly referred to in paragraph two of point 5. The FPInvA in the first paragraph of this point also speaks of the right to possess, use, and dispose of the object, although this formulation does not necessarily encompass title.

The FPInvA does not establish at what moment the investor acquires the right of ownership in an object of investment. However, paragraph two of point 5 of this Article provides for the possibility of an investor subsequently taking an object in which he has not acquired the right of ownership (see Commentary to Article 6[5]). From this we may draw the conclusion that according to the general rule an investor acquires the right of ownership at the moment when the investment is made.

In these matters the FPInvA sharply departs from Soviet civil law. The system of civil law is so structured that the application of its norms to relations which constitute an "investment" lead to the result that an investor may not always have the same rights affecting the object of investing. Various types of investment take on various civil-law forms. The last are determined by the sundry norms of civil law which regulate the particular type of relations. Therefore as a result of investing an investor is in a different legal position and possesses various rights.

Among the civil-law forms concerning investment there exists only one which leads to an investor acquiring the right of ownership in the object of investment. But even in those situations the investor is not an owner, but merely a co-owner.

That civil-law form is the purchase-sale contract for a share in the right of ownership to a thing constituting the material basis for an object of entrepreneurial activity. In such a contract the investor acts as a purchaser, and the owner of the thing as the seller. The "investment" is regulated by rules of civil law concerning the purchase-sale contract. The 1991 FPCivL provides that "under a purchase-sale contract, the seller shall be obliged to transfer property (or thing, good) to the ownership (or full economic jurisdiction or operative management) of the buyer..."[71] Since this contract governs the sale of a share in the property of an object of entrepreneurial activity, common share ownership of the investor and seller arises. This is the sole instance when the norms of civil law

---

[71]   Article 74. Translated in W. E. Butler, *The USSR Fundamental Principles of Civil Legislation* (1991). The same essential wording appeared in Article 39 of the 1961 FPCivL. Transl. in W. E. Butler (comp. & transl.), *The Soviet Legal System: Legislation and Documentation*(1978), p. 405.

endow the investor with the right of ownership to a share in property and the right to possess, use, and dispose of the object (with the consent of the seller).

All other civil-law forms governing "investment" do not entail the investor acquiring the right of ownership in the object of investment. The contract of loan is widely used in which the investor acts as the lender and the owner of the object as the borrower. The norms of civil law devoted to this contract do not give the lender the right of ownership in the borrower's property. The same is true of the contract of lease, which may govern certain instances of "investment" in movable and immovable property (buildings, installations, equipment, and other material valuables). The provisions concerning such a contract do not endow the lessor with the right of ownership in the property of the lessee. The same applies to an author's contract on the basis of which there occurs an "investment" of property rights arising from copyright: an author who has transferred a manuscript to a publishing house for publication does not become the owner of the publishing house.

The norms of civil law regulating "investment" connected with the creation by a Soviet and foreign juridical person of a joint enterprise also do not give the investor the right of ownership in the property of the object of investment. The founders contribute specified valuables to the charter fund of the enterprise, but they do not acquire the right of ownership in the property of the joint enterprise. According to the 1990 USSR Law on Ownership, the right of ownership to its property belongs to the joint enterprise itself.[72]

---

[72]   Article 27. See M. I. Braginskii, W. E. Butler, and A. A. Rubanov (commentary), *The Law on Ownership in the USSR* (1991), pp. 237-240.

Finally, the civil-law norms regulating a joint-stock society also do not transform the investor into the owner of the rights of ownership in the things of a joint-stock society when an "investment" is made by acquiring stocks. The investor acquires the right of ownership in the stock and becomes the subject of rights arising from the stock. The right of ownership, however, in the property of a joint-stock society is not acquired by an investor. According to the 1990 Statute on joint-stock societies, a society has the right of ownership in property transferred to it by its participants, to the products produced by the society as a result of economic activity, and to the revenues received and other property acquired by a society on other grounds permitted by legislation.[73] Therefore it is the joint-stock society and not the stockholders which has the right of possession, use, and disposition of all of its property.

The civil-law norms which may govern an "investment" are exceedingly diverse, and the number of examples could be multiplied manyfold. But enough has been said to justify the conclusion that the FPInvA created a unique situation in Soviet law with the present provision: the FPInvA as a law has departed materially from the established system of civil-law regulation. This can not but have consequences, although precisely what is difficult to foresee. The civil law, just as any system, is quite a stable one with a considerable reserve of forces based on a millenium of European civilist civilisation.

14. The provision of the FPInvA that an investor has the right to possess, use, and dispose of the results of investments is internally linked with the rule that any "investment" gives the investor the right of ownership in

---

[73]   Point 15. Transl. in W. E. Butler (ed.), *Basic Documents on the Soviet Legal System* (2d ed., 1991), p. 326.

the object of investment. As a basic principle, this rule diverges sharply from the entire system of civil law.

An "investment" is governed by a vast number of civil-law relations in which the investor and the recipient of the investment participate. Each type of these legal relations is regulated by special civil-law norms. Therefore the legal position of the investor with respect to the results of investment activity depends upon in which civil-law relations he is participating. There is and can not be a single position in this case.

There exists merely one civil-law form under which the right of ownership in a thing belongs to an investor and arises as a result of the use of the object of investment. This is a purchase-sale contract for a share in property forming the material base of the object of entrepreneurial activity. In this event the investor becomes a co-owner. The right of ownership in fruits and revenues generated by the thing respectively belong to him (Article 140, 1964 RSFSR Civil Code).

In all other civil-law forms which may govern an "investment" the investor does not have the right of ownership in the fruits and revenues generated by the property on which the object of entrepreneurial activity is based.

The contradiction between the norm of the FPCivL being considered here and the entire system of civil law requires resolution.

15. The FPInvA specially mentions reinvestments and trade operations on the territory of the USSR. This in and of itself is very important because serious issues arise here for foreign investors. Regrettably this has been done

in the most controversial Article of the FPInvA which is clearly contrary to the entire system of civil law. This positioning of the reference seriously weakens its legal significance.

Moreover, it is doubtful whether reinvestments and especially trade operations should be relegated to the category of the results of investments. The result of investments is the fact that certain financial and other possibilities arise for reinvestment or trade operations.

16. The FPInvA provides in point 5, paragraph two, of this Article that legislation of the USSR and republics may determine the objects, investment in which does not entail the acquisition of the right of ownership, but this does not exclude "subsequent possession" or "subsequent operative management" of an investor.

This provision does not fully accord with the rule set out in paragraph one of this same point, where it is established that an investor has the right to possess, use, and dispose of objects of investments. This allows no exceptions: the rights enumerated belong to the investor for always.

The rule contained in paragraph 2 of this point should be understood to mean that legislation of the USSR and republics may determine the objects of investment in which an investor does not acquire the right of ownership at the moment of investing. But in this event the legislation must be so structured that "subsequent possession" and "subsequent operative management" of these objects are not excluded.

This rule is ambiguous in many respects. As regards possession, this is normally understood as the actual dominion of a person over a thing. Subsequent possession as mentioned by the FPInvA is consequently the actual dominion of an investor over the property of an object of investment activity established by the investor after the "investment" was made. It is thus contemplated to issue those legislative acts which would not give an investor the right of ownership in an object of investing but would endow the investor with the right to take this object into his possession. The FPInvA leaves open the question as to how in this event the relations between the investor and the recipient of the investment should be regulated.

There is yet another instance when the FPInvA sharply diverges from the entire system of civil law. Even when an investor as the result of purchasing a share in the property of an object of entrepreneurial activity becomes the owner thereof, civil law provides that the possession of common share ownership is with the consent of all of the participants thereof (Article 117, 1964 RSFSR Civil Code). And there are no grounds for endowing an investor with the right to subsequently take an object into possession when an investment is governed by civil law.

Even more doubtful are the words of the FPInvA concerning "subsequent operative management." According to the 1990 USSR Law on Ownership, the category of "operative management" applies to property which is State ownership and allocated to a State institution on the State budget (Article 26[1]). The subsequent operative management to which the FPInv refers is presumably the operative management which occurs after the "investment" was made. In essence it is contemplated to issue legislative acts which would provide for the right of an investor to take the property of State budget institutions on the State budget.

The adoption of such laws is not expedient. One should not forget that budget institutions perform major functions in the domain of State administration. The transfer of their property to investors could have negative consequences for society as a whole.

17. As in several other places, point 6 of this Article is a literary exercise rather than a legal rule.

And as elsewhere this provision requires criticism. It is not clear why the FPInvA refers to property which is necessary for the investor. He has the right to acquire property which is necessary not for him but for a participant of investment activity who performs his orders and commissions.

The middleman or intermediary according to Soviet civil law is purely a factual figure and is created by the parties who conclude a contract between themselves. The middleman himself is not a party to the contract. Therefore from the standpoint of civil law one does not speak of the acquisition of property "through intermediaries" or "middlemen."

It must be observed that the FPInvA does not limit the sphere of its description to the territory of the Soviet Union. An investor has the right to acquire property irrespective of whether one speaks of Soviet or foreign citizens and juridical persons from whom the property is acquired.

Article 7: Relations Between Subjects of Investment Activity

1. The principal legal document regulating mutual relations between subjects of investment activity shall be the contract (or agreement).

The conclusion of contracts, the choice of partners, the determination of obligations and any other conditions of economic relations which are not contrary to legislation of the USSR and the union and autonomous republics, shall be within the exclusive competence of the subjects of investment activity. Interference of State agencies and officials in the effectuation of contractual relations between subjects of investment activity outside their competence shall not be permitted.

The subjects of investment activity shall have the right to organise tenders (or auctions) in order to attract citizens and juridical persons to effectuate investment activity.

2. The conditions of contracts concluded between subjects of investment activity shall retain their force for the entire effect of the contracts also in instances when after their conclusion conditions have been established by legislation which worsen the position of the subjects, if they have not come to an agreement about a change of conditions of the contract.

1. The FPInvA divides the subject of investment activity into two groups: investors and participants of investment activity. The FPInvA does not deem the recipients of investments to be subjects. Therefore the relations referred to in this Article are relations between investors and subjects which ensure the effectuation of investments as executors of orders or on the basis of commissions of investors (Article 4[3]).

2. The text of point 1 is not a norm of law, but an exercise in literary composition addressed to persons interested in the legal aspects of investment activity. As such, it is not adequately orientated towards moving the Soviet Union towards a market economy. The contract is the sole form of bringing together investments and the objects of entrepreneurial or other activity that is suited to the conditions existing in the investment market. The FPInvA calls the contract merely the principal means of regulating relations between subjects of investment activity.

This indicates that there may be other sources of regulation which, albeit not principal, nonetheless are of significance for the parties. When the Soviet Union is but beginning to move away from forms used in the administrative-command system, this language might be understood to suggest that, together with contract, plan also remains of importance.

3. Nor is the concept of contract advanced by the FPInvA beyond reproach. Various views on the contract have been expressed in civil law doctrine. Some believe contract is a legal fact with which the law links legal

consequences; others are of the view that contract is a form of the expression of the will of the parties, and yet others assert that it is a means of organising the agreed activity of the parties. The FPInvA offers its own definition of the contract as a "legal document;" that is, as a piece of paper with a legal text on it. At best this is merely a layman's understanding of contract.

The concept of competence used by the FPInvA applies only to agencies of power and administration, and not to subjects of civil law. The FPInvA also speaks of the competence of State agencies and officials, by virtue of which they all turn out to be on the same level.

The FPInvA pursues a laudable purpose when it prohibits State agencies and officials from interfering in the effectuation of contractual relations. But the stipulation that they are not permitted to do so in excess of their competence sounds most strange. However, if the actions of State agencies or officials are performed within their competence, this is not interference but the regulation of contractual relations.

4. The FPInvA grants the right to organise tenders or auctions. In the transition to the market economy, this provision may be of great significance. Only since 1989 has this method begun to be used extensively, but it will be a major vehicle for the privatisation of State ownership.

Even this provision is not without shortcomings. The FPInvA gives the right to organise auctions and tenders only to subjects of investment activity. The recipients of investments are not included (see Commentary to Article 4[3]). In an investment market, however, it is the recipients of investments who may be especially interested in the right to organise auctions and tenders.

The FPInvA does not attempt to determine which are the principal norms that regulate auctions and tenders nor does it establish renvoi norms specifying which legislation should regulate relations arising in this event. The right thus granted to subjects of investment activity is operating in a legal vacuum, which seriously complicates its realisation.

5. Point 2 contains a new and important rule directed towards ensuring the stability of relations regulated by the FPInvA. By virtue of this provision relations which fall within the operation of the FPInvA are placed in a much superior position vis-a-vis other civil-law relations. When intensive investment activity is underway in the Soviet Union on several levels, this provision is of particular importance. And it is especially significant for foreign investors, who are even more interested in the stability of relations and guarantees.

It should be borne in mind, though, that since the FPInvA does not regard the recipients of investments as subjects of investment activity (see Commentary to Article 4[3]) this rule extends neither to contracts concluded by an investor with the recipient of investments nor to contracts concluded by a recipient with participants of investment activity. In the latter cases general principles of law and those relevant special norms concerning the introduction into effect of specific laws operate.

Article 8: Duties of Subjects of Investment Activity

1. An investor, in the instances and procedure established by legislation of the USSR and the union and autonomous republics, shall be obliged to:

submit a declaration to financial agencies about the amounts and sources of investments effectuated by him;

receive necessary authorisations and agreement of respective agencies of power and special services for capital investment;

receive the opinion of experts on investment projects with respect to complying with sanitary-hygienic and ecological requirements.

2. Subjects of investment activity shall be obliged to:

comply with norms and standards, the procedure for the establishment of which is determined by legislation of the USSR and the union and autonomous republics;

not permit manifestations of unfair competition and to fulfil requirements of anti-monopoly legislation;

fulfil requirements of State agencies and officials presented within the limits of their competence;

submit bookkeeping and statistical reports in the established procedure.

3. Each participant of investment activity fulfilling special types of work which require appropriate attestation of performance must have a license for the right to effectuate this type of work. A list of such work and the procedure for licensing shall be established by legislation of the USSR and the union and autonomous republics within the limits of their competence.

1.   Point 1 of this Article contains rules of a renvoi character. The FPInvA does not here directly impose any duties on the investor, but merely determines which duties might be imposed thereon by legislation of the USSR or republics, the latter simultaneously being given the right determine the procedure for investors to perform those duties. The legal situation in this domain thus must await future legislation, especially of the republics (see Commentary to Article 5).

2.   When the republics adopt acts to implement these prescriptions, special problems will arise for investors who are foreign juridical persons or citizens. The imposition on them of the duty to obtain the requisite authorisations and agreements, as well as expert evaluations of investment projects, will require a vast series of measures on the territory of the USSR. The foreign investor will require the assistance of qualified jurists who are specialists in Soviet law.

3.   Special attention should be drawn to the possibility of establishing requirements by way of legislation for foreign investors to submit a declaration

concerning the amounts and sources of the investments being effectuated.

The FPInvA uses the words "amounts" and "sources" in the plural. This opens the possibility that declarations will be required not only with regard to the specific investment project, but also information regarding all investment projects of a particular foreign investor both in the USSR and abroad. Future legislation might even require a declaration concerning all financial operations of a foreign investor.

It should be stressed that the FPInvA does not contain rules which would bind financial agencies who received such information to preserve its confidentiality. Although future legislation may do so, it would have been desirable to include an appropriate provision here.

4.   Point 2 of this Article places duties directly on subjects of investment activity. Among such subjects are foreign juridical persons, foreign citizens, and foreign States who act as investors.

5.   The requirement to comply with norms and standards is of importance to foreign investors because there are many thousands of standards and conditions which have been established by Gosstroi SSSR and which apply to capital construction. The provision on anti-monopoly legislation had in view enactments then under consideration and adopted by the USSR and republics beginning in March 1991.

6. The duty to submit bookkeeping records is of great importance for foreign investors. The Soviet Union still has no system of public accounts for juridical persons. Except for joint enterprises created under Decree No. 49 of 13 January 1987, for whom a series of bookkeeping regulations has brought their requirements closer to international standards, basic bookkeeping activities are regulated by the Statute on Bookkeeping Accounts and Balance Sheets as amended and the Statute on the Chief Bookkeeper. One should bear in mind that since 1928 a procedure has been operative in the USSR whereby the chief bookkeeper in enterprises was juxtaposed against the director of the enterprise to a certain extent as a kind of State controller over compliance with instructions relating to carrying on economic activities. The chief bookkeeper even had a right of veto over certain decisions by virtue of his so-called "right of second signature."

In business circles the view has been expressed that this procedure ought to be done away with. Only the owner or director of an enterprise accountable to the owner (or stockholders, cooperative members, etc.) should bear responsibility for the state of affairs in an enterprise. It is proposed to give the director of an enterprise a freedom of choice: to keep the books himself, or conclude a contract with a specialised firm to do so, or to appoint a chief bookkeeper who would head up the accounting division within the enterprise.[74]

But this is merely a proposal. The 1990 USSR Law on taxes from enterprises, associations, and organisations provides that "payers of taxes ... shall be obliged ... to keep bookkeeping records and reports in the established procedure concerning financial and economic activities

---

[74]   *Ekonomika i zhizn'*, no. 51 (1990,) p. 11.

and submit bookkeeping reports and balance sheets ... to tax agencies.[75]

7.   Point 3 of this Article is linked with the changes which have occurred in the Soviet Union as alternative non-State organisations have come into being in order to compete with massive specialist State construction, assembly, and design-survey enterprises.

The FPInvA expressly places on participants of investment activity the duty to obtain a license if they perform special types of work requiring that the performer of that work be attested. In and of itself the provision is reasonable and essential. However, the FPInvA does not establish that such licenses should be issued by an impartial State body. There is merely a renvoi norm indicating that the procedure for the issuance of licenses must be established by other legislative acts of the Union and the republics.

The question may become crucial if the Soviet Union continues in the direction of a market economy. It should be noted that when export licenses were introduced in the domain of foreign trade, the right to issue the licenses was in many cases granted to those State agencies which were responsible for directing the vast group of enterprises who produced the product concerned. Those institutions often abused their right and refused export licenses in order to protect their own enterprises against competition from others.

---

[75]   Article 36(1). Transl. in W. E. Butler (ed.), *Basic Documents on the Soviet Legal System* (2d ed., 1991) p. 455. This Article is not affected by subsequent amendments to the Law as consolidated in the text of 11 June 1991. See *Izvestiia*, 22 June 1991, p. 3, cols. 1-6

The silence of the FPInvA on this point means this domain of activity is not protected against similar policies.

Article 9: Sources of Financing Investment Activity

Investment activity may be effectuated at the expense of:

the financial resources of the investor himself (profit, amortisation deductions, cash accumulations, savings of citizens, juridical persons, and others);

borrowed financial assets of investors (bonds, bank and budget credits);

invested financial assets of the investor (assets obtained from the sale of stocks, shares, and other contributions of citizens and juridical persons);

budget investment appropriations.

1.   The title of this Article is not consistent with its content. The FPInvA establishes that investment activity represents all the actions relating to the realisation of investments and that investments are all types of property and intellectual valuables (see Articles 1 and 2). The title of this Article suggests that it will set out the sources for financing all such activity. The promise is unfulfilled, especially if one takes into account that investing here should include that made by foreign citizens, foreign juridical persons, and even foreign States and international organisations (see Article 2[2] FPInvA). Consequently, the task assumed by this Article has truly global dimensions.

Happily, the legislator confined himself to enumerating certain sources of financing such investment activity when the investor is a State enterprise.

These sources are divided by the FPInvA into four types: one's own, borrowed, and attracted assets of the investor, as well as budget investment appropriations.

It is doubtful whether the investor's own financial resources should be juxtaposed with budget investment appropriations. The FPInvA provides that State investing is effectuated by agencies of power and administration of the USSR and the union and autonomous republics, autonomous regions and national areas, and other administrative-territorial formations and expressly stipulate that such investing is "at the expense of budget assets" (Article 2[2]). For the investors enumerated the respective assets are their own, and therefore there is no basis for juxtaposing budget investment appropriations with the investor's financial resources.

2. Among the innovations contained in this provision is the reference to budget credits. This is a move away from budget investing which is not to be repaid, for the latter was one of the reasons for the economic difficulties being experienced by the Soviet Union. It remains to be seen how extensively State agencies which distribute budget appropriations will engage in credit operations and how such activities will be coordinated with bank activities and policies.

Section III: State Regulation of Investment Activity

Investment Activity

Article 10:   Purposes and Forms of State Regulation of Investment Activity

1.   State regulation of investment activity shall be effectuated for the purposes of realising economic, scientific-technical, and social policies. It shall be determined by plans and programmes for the development of the national economy confirmed by the USSR Supreme Soviet and by the union and autonomous republic supreme soviets, by the budgets of the USSR and the union and autonomous republics, and by the amounts of State financing provided therein.

Preferential conditions shall be created in this connection for investors who effectuate investment activity in directions most important for the satisfaction of social requirements and, above all, in the social sphere, technical improvement of production, and the introduction of discoveries and inventions.

2.   State regulation of investment activity shall include the regulation of conditions of investment activity and the direct administration of State investments.

1.   Point 1 of this Article does not fully correspond to the breadth of investment activity as set out in Section I of the FPInvA (see Commentary to Articles 1 and 2). But for Article 19, all the Articles in this Section are devoted to capital construction, and only to that capital

construction effectuated at the expense of the Union budget. And in this domain the FPInvA retains intact to a considerable degree the administrative-planning principles which always have been most severe in the domain of capital construction.

2. The purposes of State regulation of investment activity in Point 1 have been defined broadly. Everything said in this connection could in equal measure appertain to any activity carried on in the Soviet Union. For this reason one might conclude that the provisions here have no special significance for those who are to apply the FPInvA (including agencies of administration who organised civil turnover within the framework of their competence, enterprises and organisations which participate therein, as well as jurisdictional organs which settle disputes within the limits of their competence that arise in connection with the effectuation of investment activity). For these reasons of excessive generality, this point can not be directly applied, even when a jurisdictional organ renders a decision on the basis of analogy of law [*pravo*][76]

3. Meriting special attention is the fact that State regulation encompasses the entire sphere of investment activity irrespective of whether it is effectuated by State, cooperative, or social organisations or enterprises or by citizens and irrespective of whether it is made from funds which belong to the investor himself or funds obtained by him at a bank[77] in the form of loans, or from budget

---

[76]   By virtue of Article 12, FPCivProc, in the absence of a law [*zakon*] regulating a relation in dispute, the court applies the law [*zakon*] regulating a similar relation (analogy of *zakon*), and in the absence of the latter, the court proceeds from the general principles and meaning of Soviet legislation (analogy of *pravo*).

[77]   The State monopoly of banking which existed until recently was reflected in the

appropriations. The legal regime of the effectuation of investment activity by various subjects of turnover, previously differentiated, is now virtually merged. This enables one to conclude that in the course of perestroika there is a clear trend towards ultimately establishing a unified legal regime for investment activity irrespective of who invests and how.

4. In allowing the possibility that respective relations may be regulated by various acts issued by competent State agencies, paragraph one of Point 1 of this Article consolidated the priority of *zakon*. This is of great importance for that part of economic legislation which regulates relations formed in the course of investment activity. So-called subordinate acts -- decrees of the Government of the USSR, orders and instructions of USSR ministries and departments (and in significantly

---

fact that in addition to the USSR State Bank, which was simultaneously a clearing, credit, and emissive centre and was together with its institutions (or branches) a unified legal person, there existed investment (so-called "special" banks) created as far back as 1932 for long-term investments. These last were the Trade Bank of the USSR, the Industrial Bank of the USSR, the Agricultural Bank of the USSR, as well as municipal banks. Eventually all special banks were replaced by the Construction Bank of the USSR. Investment banks belonged to the State. They were called upon to ensure the financial servicing of investors in the respective economic sphere. Three investment banks -- Trade, Industrial, and Agricultural -- were similar to the USSR State Bank, a unified legal person. Their branches situated in various areas of the Soviet Union respectively acted in the name of the respective bank of the USSR. However, the municipal banks comprised a system of legally and economically autonomous bank institutions distributed throughout the Soviet Union. See E. A. Fleishits, *Raschetno-kreditnye pravootnosheniia* (1956), p. 127ff. Under perestroika the USSR has renounced its State monopoly of bank activities. The legislation in force in this domain, especially the Laws of the USSR "On the State Bank of the USSR" and "On Banks and Bank Activities" adopted 11 December 1990 proceed from the fact that together with the State banks (besides the USSR State Bank there also are central banks of the republics which have received autonomy, including recognition as legal persons), commercial banks are functioning. Among the latter are those in which foreign capital is participating, by which is meant banks structured as a joint enterprise with the participation of foreign and national capital simultaneously, as well as those created exclusively by a foreign investor. In the latter two instances a foreign bank must be at least one of the founders. See *Vedomosti SND SSSR* (1990) no. 52, items 1154-1155

lower quantities, the analogous acts of republic governments, ministries, and departments) constitute the overwhelming majority of enactments in this branch of economic legislation. Such basic enactments as the Rules on Independent-Work Contracts in Capital Construction and the Rules of Financing and Crediting Construction were confirmed by the USSR Council of Ministers, and the principal act regulating relations of customers and those who perform work in the domain of new technology, the Statute on Contracts for the Creation (or Transfer) of Scientific-Technical Products, was confirmed by the State Committee of the USSR for Science and Technology (see Commentary to Article 16). Among departmental acts, those emanating from the State Construction Committee of the USSR (Gosstroi SSSR) had wide application. By virtue of the decree of the USSR Council of Ministers of 2 November 1984 "On Clarifying the Functions of Gosstroi SSSR,"[78] this agency had the right to issue with regard to a series of questions specified in the Decree acts binding upon all ministries, departments, associations, organisations, and enterprises irrespective of their subordination. Despite the measures taken going back as far as 1975 to reduce the number of acts devoted to investment activity, their numbers diminished but slightly.[79] The by no means complete collection of legislation on capital construction issued in the 1980s amounted to more than ten large volumes.

The agencies mentioned in the preceding paragraph -- the USSR Council of Ministers, the USSR State Committee for Science and Technology, and Gosstroi -- were abolished or reorganised in April 1991. The status of their enactments is obscure, and in any event those

---

[78]   *SP SSSR* (1984), no. 22, item 119.

[79]   See M. I. Braginskii, *Sovershenstvovanie zakonodatel'stva o kapital'nom stroitel'stve* (1982), p. 12.

enactments must be read against the 1991 FPCivL, which transforms capital construction and scientific-technical contracts.

5. The specific list of privileges mentioned in paragraph two of Point 1 of this Article and the procedure for applying them have been provided for in various acts. An example is the Rules for Financing and Crediting Construction confirmed by the USSR Council of Ministers on 10 January 1987.[80] They provide that to enterprises which successfully fulfil construction plans there apply incentive measures such as reduction of bank interest on loans, the release of budget assets in advance of schedule, and the like. Of a different nature are privileges connected with the allocation of land plots: the local soviet may within the limits of its competence grant enterprises (or associations), organisations, and institutions which are part of the local economy[81] a preferential right to use local land and other naturalresources or to material-technical supply from local funds.

6. A number of privileges connected with investment activity have been provided for by tax legislation. Thus, when calculating the tax on profit, 30% of expenditures by an enterprise for scientific-research or experimental construction design work, or for nature protection measures, does not fall within taxable profit.

---

[80]   *SP SSSR* (1987), no. 7, item 31.

[81]   The local economy includes enterprises, organisations, institutions, and objects of production and social infrastructure which are the ownership of the administrative-territorial entity itself, as well as other enterprises and organisations whose activity is connected primarily with servicing the populace. The last, in cases when the owners of the enterprise or association have agreed to do so.

7. Point 2 of this Article proceeds from the existence of two forms of organised activity of competent State agencies: first, the adoption of abstract norms (new laws, decrees, and the like) and second, the issuance of administrative acts, that is, those which have in view specific participants of turnover and directly give rise to specified rights and duties on the part of addressees (a planning act binding upon the parties is an example of the latter).

8. The provisions of Point 2 of this Article are further clarified in Articles 11 and 12 (see Commentary below).

Article 11: State Regulation of Conditions of Investment Activity

State regulation of the conditions of investment activity shall be effectuated by agencies of the USSR and the union and autonomous republics in accordance with legislation by:

the system of taxes with differentiation of subjects and objects of taxation, tax rates, and privileges. A differential tax on investments may be introduced by the USSR Supreme Soviet and by the union and autonomous republic supreme soviets for the purposes of regulating investment demand;

amortisation policy, including by accelerated amortisation of basic funds. In this connection privileges relating to amortisation may be established differentially for individual branches and spheres of the economy, elements of basic funds, and types of equipment;

granting financial assistance in the form of grants, subsidies, subventions, and budget loans for the development of individual regions, branches, and production entities;

means of effectuating credit policy, State norms and standards, anti-monopoly measures, privatisation of State ownership, including unfinished construction, and price-formation policy;

conditions for the use of land and other natural resources;

expert evaluation of investment projects.

Extrabudgetary investment funds formed in the procedure established by legislative acts of the USSR and the union and autonomous republics, as well as funds for the support of small enterprises, may be used as economic methods of State regulation of investment activity.

1. This Article is principally concerned with defining the various methods of regulating the conditions of investment activity. The majority of them are economic in character and thus are consolidated by a dispositive norm whose aim is to interest the participants of turnover in choosing that variant which is optimal from the standpoint of they themselves and the State as a whole. Several provisions (though a clear minority) contemplate the establishment by a State agency of binding norms, thereby precluding the possibility of choice by the participants of turnover.

2. One of the principal legal sources regulating the system of taxes (see paragraph two of this Article) is the 1990 USSR Law of 14 June 1990 on taxes from enterprises, associations, and organisations.[82] The Law extends to both Soviet organisations and joint enterprises created on the territory of the USSR with the participation of Soviet juridical persons and citizens as well as foreign juridical persons and citizens, international associations which effectuate economic activity, branches domiciled in the USSR of joint enterprises situated abroad and created with the participation of Soviet organisations, and

---

[82]   *Vedomosti SND SSSR* (1990), no. 19, item 320; transl. in W. E. Butler (ed.), *Basic Documents on the Soviet Legal System* (2d ed., 1991), pp. 409-461. The Law has been amended since its original enactment.

international nongovernmental organisations or associations provided that they receive revenues from economic and other commercial activities. The Law is concerned only with all-union taxes: tax on profit, turnover tax, tax on export and import, tax on the growth of consumption assets, and tax on revenues. The Law devotes a special chapter to each type of tax, and each chapter differs from the others not only by object (which is how the taxes are differentiated from one another) but also by groups of juridical persons. For example, the payers of turnover tax are only those enterprises which produce and realise goods or products levied with turnover tax;[83] the tax on revenues does not extend to revenues of foreign juridical persons which are not connected with their activities in the USSR, and the like. Tax privileges also are applicable to specified categories of taxpayers (there are no special privileges in the chapter devoted to the tax on export and import).

Union tax legislation has been supplemented by republic enactments. An example is the RSFSR Law of 1 December 1990 devoted to the application of the Union Law on taxes on the territory of the Russian Federation.[84] The RSFSR Law contains many norms which differ materially from those in the Union Law: for example, the rates for individual types of taxes in many instances introduce additional privileges for individual categories of taxpayers (such as enterprises engaged in design and construction or in the reconstruction of major highways). According to the RSFSR Law, the right to determine the conditions of introducing and the rates of turnover tax has

---

[83]   In a number of cases the 1990 USSR tax law on enterprises is supplemented by Statutes enacted for individual types of taxes. The Statute on the Turnover Tax, for example, was confirmed by the USSR Council of Ministers on 29 December 1990, Decree No. 1358, with effect from 1 January 1991. See *SP SSSR* (1991) I, no. 3, item 13.

[84]   *Vedomosti SND RSFSR* (1990) no. 29, item 384.

been granted to the RSFSR Council of Ministers, whereas according to the USSR Law only the Government of the USSR has this right. Here there was a clear conflict of all-union and republic legislation whose resolution ultimately awaited the Treaty of the Union (see Commentary to Article 18).

3. The amortisation deductions referred to in paragraph 3 of this Article are directed towards actively renewing the basic funds and accelerating scientific-technical progress, reducing expenditures for capital repair of physically worn-out machines, equipment, and means of transport. Having in view the exceptional importance of these problems for the transition to the market economy, the USSR Council of Ministers introduced with effect from 1 January 1991 Unified Norms of Amortisation Deductions for the Full Restoration of Basic Funds. In confirming these norms, the USSR Council of Ministers included in the decree a number of very important provisions. Amortisation deductions for full restoration of basic funds (or machines, equipment, and means of transport) must be made within the normative period of their service or the period for which their balance sheet value as a whole is carried over to production and circulation expenses. Moreover, expenses for all types of repair of basic funds is included in expenditures for the production and realisation of a product, that is, its cost of production. The respective amounts thereby become an element of the price of the produce, work, or service and consequently are paid by the consumer.

The Statute confirmed by the decree establishes a number of unified norms providing for the privileges mentioned in this paragraph of the Article. The

Government of the USSR considered it necessary to allow "accelerated amortisation" with respect to the technically more important basic funds. The decree itself merely mentions basic funds used to increase the production of computer technology, new progressive materials, instruments, and equipment, as well as for the expansion of export products. The State Planning Committee, abolished in March 1991, was granted the right to expand the list of items subject to accelerated amortisation.

Certain privileges were narrowly drawn. Higher amortisation rates, for example, apply for cable communications in the Far North, the Far East, permafrost areas, Iakutia, and Magadan.

The Unified Norms are addressed expressly to Soviet organisations. But joint enterprises with foreign participation registered in the USSR, unless provided otherwise by their charters, are governed by the amortisation norms applicable to Soviet State enterprises. Joint enterprises thus have the right to determine the amounts of amortisation deductions themselves, and only if they fail to do so are the Unified Norms applicable.

4. Paragraph four of this Article, devoted to financial assistance, distinguishes among grants, subventions, subsidies, and budget loans. They share in common the fact that they have as their subject cash assets of a superior budget directed towards an inferior budget link; that is, assets granted by one owner to another (the USSR to a union republic; a union republic to an autonomous republic; a union or autonomous republic to territories, regions, cities, etc.).

Grants and subsidies appear for the first time in the FPInvA. Previously one spoke about the transfer of revenues allocated to a superior budget level down to a lower level either in full or in part.

Subventions were used in the early years after the Soviet Revolution in 1917 and in recent years have been taken up again. The 1990 USSR Law on the State Budget provided for subventions to five union republics, especially to contribute to equalisation of the levels of social security for the populace and to pay compensation for differential price levels amongst regions of the Soviet Union.

More widely used are special-purpose nonrepayable appropriations to inferior budgets specifying the specific purposes for which the money is to be spent. The 1990 USSR State Budget allocated, for example, 100 million rubles for repair and restorative work relating to the agro-chemical complex which had suffered from earthquakes.

Budget loans are a new source of investment, and not yet the subject of normative regulation. USSR legislation does not even mention the forms of rendering assistance to inferior budgets. The first mention appears in republic enactments. The RSFSR Law "On Forming Budgets in the RSFSR in 1991" made provision for the forming of special-purpose funds in order to finance unforeseen and extraordinary measures according to a republic programme and also for subventions and subsidies to budgets in the RSFSR; these are to be financed from State taxes and revenues received in the republic budget and from other sources (Article 8).

5. "Credit policy" here refers to the establishment of the basic principles of giving credits. The granting of credits should be repayable, periodic (that is, periods for

repayment should be fixed), secured (by various forms of pledge), and for compensation (payment of interest on the loan). Until recently the principles of directive planning prevailed, and credits were correspondingly issued only when the planning prerequisites were present: credit ceilings established for each participant of economic turnover. In a few instances strictly defined by applicable rules, credits were provided without ceilings; for all practical purposes this approach to providing credits has ceased to be used both in commercial and State banks. However, when these principles were employed, they were generally binding on both State and all other types of banks.

6.   The regulation of investment activity in a number of instances is reflected in the establishment of a variety of normative standards by competent agencies. For the most part, these are economic normative standards whose purpose is to ensure throughout their period of operation the linkage between general State interests and the interests of enterprises. Such normative standards must enable the creation of conditions under which an enterprise will be interested in accepting offers from a contracting party which are the optimum variants from the standpoint of the national economy and, no less important, are economically advantageous to the contracting party.

Of enormous importance for capital construction are the State standards confirmed either by the State Committee of the USSR for Construction and Investments (as renamed) or by the Committee of Standardisation and Metrology of the USSR (as renamed), as well as construction norms and rules confirmed by the Statute Committee of the USSR for Construction and Investments.[15] There are more than 100 State standards and in excess of 10,000 construction norms and rules. Both contain legal rules together with purely technical ones, and there are both Union and republic standards which differ from one another. Both contain binding and recommendatory provisions.

Binding provisions are allowed only when provided for by law (these principally are safety and environmental requirements). These binding provisions of the standards extend to all participants of civil turnover, including both Soviet and foreign joint enterprises with foreign participation and wholly-owned foreign enterprises in the Soviet Union. The recommendatory provisions need be complied with only on condition that a contract so provides. An enterprise may, moreover, established standards itself if they are stricter than the respective Union or republic standard. International, regional, and even foreign standards may have direct effect in the Soviet Union if two conditions are satisfied: first, their application is based on an international treaty of the USSR; and second, the standard is capable of satisfying the requirements of the national economy of the USSR[86]

Construction norms and rules (CNR) establish the basic requirements for design and construction. Among others are those which contain norms concerning the allotment of land, the duration of the design and construction of objects, the expenditure of construction materials, sanitation requirements of industrial enterprises, electrical installations, technical design requirements, and others.

---

[85]   These bodies were renamed by Decree No. 176 of the USSR Council of Ministers adopted 13 April 1991. See *Pravitel'stvennyi vestnik*, no. 17 (1991) p. 5.

[86]   See D. E. Tiagai and A. D. Romanov, *Zakonodatel'stvo o standartizatsii. Sostoianie, Problemy, Perspektivy* (1988).

7. The procedure for effectuating privatisation referred to in paragraph five of this Article is regulated principally on the USSR level by a Law on privatisation and destatisation adopted in July 1991[87] and similar republic enactments.[88] The distinction between "destatisation" and "privatisation" is crucial. The first represents the transformation of a State enterprise into an enterprise based on non-State forms of ownership, whereas the second is the transformation into the ownership of citizens of all or part of the stocks or shares of joint-stock societies and other economic societies and partnerships, as well as the sale to citizens of enterprises based on State or collective ownership. It is evident that this paragraph of the FPInvA contemplates both destatisation and privatisation.

8. On price formation, referred to in paragraph five of this Article, see the Commentary to Article 19.

9. The conditions for the use of land and other natural resources, paragraph three of this Article, are regulated by special enactments for each type of natural resource. Of these, the enactments concerning land are of greatest importance.

Before the enactment of the USSR Law "On the State Enterprise (or Association) in the USSR"[89] the Soviet

---

[87]   See the Law on the Fundamental Principles of Destaisation and Privatisation of Enterprises. *Izvestia*, 8 August 1991, pp. 3-4.

[88]   See the RSFSR Law on Privatisation of State and Municipal Enterprises in the RSFSR, of 3 July 1991. *Sovetskaia Rossiia*, 17 July 1991, pp. 3-4.

[89]   *Vedomosti SSSR* (1987), no. 26, item 395; (1989) no. 9, item 214; this Law was deemed to have lost force on 7 March 1991, together with the amendments thereto of 3 August 1989. See *Vedomosti SND SSSR* (1991), no. 12, item 325.

Union systematically granted natural resources for use without payment. That Law, however, imposed on enterprises the duty to pay for the natural resources which

they used, and the USSR land, water, and minerals legislation then in force was amended respectively.⁹⁰ The approach of the amendment was interesting: to the provision that the use of respective natural resources would be free of charge an addition was made to the effect that by way of exception the USSR Council of Ministers might provide for instances when the use of the respective resources would be for payment.

New legislation on natural resources has not yet been submitted for debate. The 1990 FPLand⁹¹ together with the 1989 FPLease⁹² and republic land codes⁹³ and laws, have materially changed the regime of land use. The basic principles are as follows:

- land is granted either for "possession" or for "use." Both terms are used in the FPLand conditionally, which is apparent when one takes into account that the possession of land (that is, the generally understood notion of de facto ownership of a thing) is combined with use (the satisfaction of any requirements by the thing), and the use

---

⁹⁰   The relevant sets of Fundamental Principles prior to their amendment are translated in W. E. Butler (comp. & transl.), *The Soviet Legal System: Legislation and Documentation* (1978), pp. 465-538.

⁹¹   Adopted 28 February 1990. *Vedomosti SND SSSR* (1990) no. 10, item 129; *Izvestiia*, 6 March 1991, p. 3, cols. 1-2. Transl. as enacted in W. E. Butler (ed.), *Basic Documents on the Soviet Legal System* (2d ed., 1991), pp. 247-268.

⁹²   Adopted 23 November 1989 and amended 7 March 1991. *Vedomosti SND SSSR* (1989) no. 25, item 481; (1991) no. 12, item 325. Transl. as originally enacted in W. E. Butler (ed.), *Basic Documents on the Soviet Legal System* (2d ed., 1991), pp. 285-300.

⁹³   Several republics have adopted land codes or laws: among them, the Belorussian SSR on 11 December 1990 (*Vedomosti BSSR* (1991), no. 2, item 11) the Kazakh SSR (*Kazakhstanskaia Pravda*, 10-11 January 1991) the RSFSR on 25 April 1991 (*Rossiiskaia gazeta*, 23 May 1991, pp. 3-7; the Turkmen SSR on 12 October 1990 (*Turkmenskaia gazeta*, 2 November 1990, pp. 1-2)

of land as a rule presupposes the simultaneous possession thereof. The essence of the difference between "possession" and "use" from the standpoint of the FPLand is to be found in its description of the powers acquired by a land possessor, on one hand, and a land user, on the other. For the most part, the powers coincide, but there are differences. One is that the land possessor has the right to autonomously decide the question of granting the plot allocated to him wholly or partially for the use of third persons. The land user must obtain the prior consent of the local soviet on those territory the plot is located, so that the group of persons to whom land is transferred in possession may be limited.

Also limited are the purposes for which land is transferred in possession. Land is granted to citizens for peasant economy, the construction of a dwelling house, dacha construction, and certain other purposes provided by the FPLand, and in all these cases the grant is inheritable possession for life. Land may be transferred to collective farms, State farms, and other State, cooperative, and social organisations for permanent possession, but only to carry on agriculture and forestry.

Some republics, such as Armenia and the RSFSR, permit peasants to acquire land in private ownership. The 1990 RSFSR Law on Ownership,[94] accompanied by respective constitutional amendments, and the 1991 RSFSR Land Code recognise private ownership as a special type of ownership and authorise such ownership for agriculture, home construction, gardening, and kitchen-gardening. The 1990 USSR Law on Ownership made no mention whatever of private ownership as such, referring merely to the "ownership of citizens."[95] However,

[94]   Adopted 24 December 1990. *Vedomosti SND RSFSR* (1990), no. 30, item 416; transl. in M. I. Braginskii, W. E. Butler, and A. A. Rubanov (commentary), *The Law on Ownership in the USSR* (1991), pp. 315-392.

the Basic Orientations of the Stabilisation of the National Economy and the Transfer to a Market Economy" adopted by the USSR Supreme Soviet on 19 October 1990 did provide that the question of private land ownership should be decided by the will of the people and specifically used the expression "private" ownership.[96] Allowing private ownership of land would mean extending to citizens, especially peasants, not only possession and use, but also the third power under the classical Roman law triad of rights: disposition.

Land use might be either permanent or temporary. Virtually all participants of turnover might be allowed the use of land: Soviet State, cooperative, and social organisations; agencies of State power and administration; joint enterprises with the participation of foreign capital; international associations and organisations with the participation of Soviet and foreign juridical persons and citizens.

The group of those to whom land might be transferred for temporary use would be even broader: in addition to the above, possible land users might include foreign States, international organisations, and foreign juridical persons and citizens. Thus a joint enterprise with the participation of foreign capital might receive a land plot either for temporary or for permanent use, and an enterprise created exclusively by a foreign investor, only for temporary use.

Temporary use of land is called a "lease" in the FPLand. The relations between lessor and lessee are fixed in the contract of lease which they conclude.

---

[95]   See M. I. Braginskii, W. E. Butler, and A. A. Rubanov (commentary), *The Law on Ownership in the USSR* (1991), pp. 81-108.

[96]   *Vedomosti SND SSSR* (1990), no. 44, item 906.

The FPLand proclaims land to be the weal of the peoples residing thereon. The substance of this provision is elaborated in other Union and republic acts. While the formulations differ, they each presuppose the triad of the rights of an owner (possession, use, and disposition) with respect to land belonging to the soviets of people's deputies (in some laws the union republic itself is deemed to be the land owner). Irrespective of how the matter is resolved in one republic or another, the power of disposition over land plots is exercised directly by the local soviet of people's deputies at the respective administrative-territorial level. In Moscow, for example, the right to grant land plots belongs to the Moscow City Soviet itself and not to the district soviets in Moscow. Juridical persons and citizens who have the right to land in possession or in use or lease treat with the local soviet in land relations.

Land possession in the USSR is for payment, recovered in the form of a land tax or lease payment. The amount of the tax is determined, taking into account the quality and location of the plot, by republic legislation, and the lease payment is determined by the contract of lease concluded between the lessor-soviet of people's deputies and the lessee. If a land plot is subleased (for example, a Soviet organisation which has received land in permanent use transfers part of its plot on lease to a joint enterprise), the amount is fixed in the sublease contract.

The FPLease contains a number of important guarantees for lessees. One is expressed in a preferential right for the lessee to renew the lease contract. This right may not be limited and thus may be protected by a lessee irrespective of whether the lessor intends to transfer the land plot to a third person or to use it for his own needs.

Amongst the legislative guarantees important for a land possessor and a land user are the provisions that their rights may be terminated compulsorily only in the instances specified in the law itself: when land is not used for its purpose; systematic failure to pay the land tax and/or lease rent; or exceeding the periods within which land must be used.

A special case is the withdrawal of a land plot for State and social needs. This requires not merely the decision of a local soviet, but also the consent of the land user or land possessor; moreover, another plot of equal value must be immediately provided. The organisation which proposes to take over the withdrawn land is obliged at its own expense to construct a building or installation equal in value to that on the plot and to compensate the former land possessor or land user for all losses caused by the withdrawal, including lost advantage. The land possessor or land user from whom a plot is to be withdrawn may protect his rights in a court. Finally, there is another peculiarity of Soviet land legislation to be noted. It consistently works from the principle that: land plot-affiliation of building or installation built thereon. This means the purchaser of a building or installation automatically receives the right to the land plot on which it is situated.

Unlike the FPLand, the Fundamental Principles on water and minerals legislation continue to follow the old formula: the normal practice is to grant for use without payment. This approach is clearly obsolete and contrary to that upon which the FPLand is built. Doubtless it will change when Union and republic legislation on water and minerals is reworked. Finally, it should be noted that although the principle of payment for natural resources was introduced into the initial 1977 redaction of the FPForest[97] and subsequent union republic forestry laws and

---

[97]   *Vedomosti SSSR* (1977), no. 25, item 388; transl. in W. E. Butler (comp. & transl.),

codes, these enactments likewise are obsolete and will be replaced.

10. The penultimate paragraph of this Article singles out amongst other forms of regulating investment activity the use of expert evaluation of investment projects. See the Commentary to Article 15.

11. The last paragraph of this Article has in view centralised funds and reserves which are created in ministries or departments and other agencies superior to enterprises.

The 1990 USSR Law on Enterprises grants to enterprises the right to participate in the formation of extrabudgetary special-purpose financial funds of the republics and local soviets of people's deputies.[98] Such participation must be strictly voluntary. Amortisation deductions of an enterprise may be the source of the respective funds. Investments within the system of the respective ministry or department are effected from the said funds and reserves.

12. The small enterprises referred to in the last paragraph of this Article are a new economic and legal category in Soviet legislation. Those enterprises are "small" where the number of workers does not exceed the maximum figure set down for particular branches of activity or industry, ranging from 200 to as low as fifteen.[99]

The Soviet Legal System: Legislation and Documentation (1978) pp. 499-520.

[98]   *Vedomosti SND SSSR* (1990) no. 25, item 461; transl. in W. E. Butler (ed.), *Basic Documents on the Soviet Legal System* (2d ed., 1991,) pp. 301-322.

[99]   See the Decree of the USSR Council of Ministers "On Measures Relating to the

Small enterprises are called upon to play an important role in increasing the number and quality of consumer goods and services, overcoming branch and regional monopolies, expanding competition and introducing new science and technology, increasing exports, providing employment for citizens, and others.

The opportunity to create small enterprises has been granted to all participants of turnover, including joint enterprises with the participation of foreign capital, State, cooperative, and social organisations, and citizens or their families. The State has expressed a special concern for such enterprises, manifested particularly in the simplified procedure for creating them, giving them full economic autonomy is carrying on their economic activities, and offering various other privileges. Amongst the latter, profit directed towards the construction, reconstruction, or renewal of basic funds, the mastery of new technology, the training and retraining of personnel, and other objects is exempt from taxation in full or in part. Moreover, the tax rates for small enterprises are lower in general than for ordinary enterprises during the first two years of their creation. Small enterprises for the production and processing of agricultural products, the production of consumer goods, and reconstruction of the production of construction materials, among others are exempted in full from profit tax for the two-year period.

It should be specially emphasised that the State has assumed the duty to render direct financial assistance to small enterprises, and this explains why the fund mentioned in this paragraph of the Article is to be created.

Creation and Development of Small Enterprises." *SP SSSR* (1990) no. 16, item 98.

Article 12: Direct Administration of State Investments

Direct administration of State investments shall be effectuated by State agencies of the USSR, union and autonomous republics, autonomous national areas and regions, and local soviets of people's deputies and shall include the planning, determination of the conditions of, and effectuation of specific actions relating to the investing of budget assets and extrabudgetary funds, and other assets attracted on a voluntary basis.

1. The operation of this Article encompasses investment activity effectuated only in the State sphere. Three financial sources are singled out as applicable: first, budget assets; second, extrabudgetary assets (having in mind, especially, revenues received by budget organisations; for example, when a university which is on the budget organises entertainment for which an admission charge is imposed)[100] and third, other assets transferred on a voluntary basis and centralised funds created by a ministry (or department) from deductions made by enterprises of its system. The failure to mention the most important source -- a State enterprise's own assets -- is evidently to be explained by the fact that such enterprises already have the right to autonomously dispose of their monetary assets. No interference of superior agencies whatever, including in the form of direct administration of State investments, is permitted.

---

[100]   A budget institution which receives revenues has the right to spend them in strict accordance with the estimate confirmed by a financial agency.

2. This Article distinguishes among several forms of administering investments on the part of agencies of State power and administration: one is norm-creation (having in view the determination of the conditions of investment), and the other two are purely administrative: first, direct actions aimed at investing (having in view chiefly the allocation of assets for capital investments) and second, planning. To each of these forms are devoted special Articles or points of individual Articles of the FPInvA (see the Commentary to Article 2(1), Article 13, and Article 14(2) and (3)).

3. This Article is of a declarative nature and accordingly in and of itself does not exert a regulating effect on the behaviour of either the organisers or participants of investment activity.

Article 13: Interaction of USSR, Union and Autonomous Republics, and Local Soviets of People's Deputies in Investment Activity

The interaction of the USSR, union and autonomous republics, and local soviets of people's deputies in investment activity shall be effectuated by:

the USSR through working out jointly with the republics the long-term socio-economic development of the country, drawing up and realising Union programmes, forming jointly with agencies of the union and autonomous republics on a voluntary basis funds for regional development, reserve, innovation, nature protection, and other all-union funds in order to finance all-union and inter-republic scientific-technical, economic, social, agrarian, nature protection, and other programmes, as well as work relating to the prevention and liquidation of the consequences of natural disasters, catastrophes, and wrecks;

union and autonomous republics through participation in the working out of general-State programmes for the development of the economy and ways of realising them, as well as the regulation of investment activity on the territory of the republic while complying with legislative acts of the USSR and union republics. Union and autonomous republics shall establish on their territory within the limits of their competence the procedure for the effectuation and ensure the protection of investments;

local soviets of people's deputies through the working out of and confirmation of socio-economic

development plans for the territory within the limits of their powers, as well as through agreeing questions relating to the creation of economic and social objects, the use of natural resources, and protection of the natural environment on the respective territory.

1. This Article, together with certain others in Section III of the FPInvA, and also recently adopted acts, determine anew the competence of the USSR, the union and autonomous republics, and local soviets of people's deputies in the sphere of planning.[101]

Before the 1990 USSR Law on Ownership entered into force, there existed a unified all-State property fund. This meant that State property, which amounted to more than 90% of Soviet production funds, belonged to only one subject -- the Soviet State as such. Acting in the name of the unified and sole subject of the law of State ownership, the highest agencies of State power and administration had the possibility of planning the national economy as a whole in the form of generally binding acts and especially the activity of State enterprises. The USSR Supreme Soviet respectively confirmed the State plan for economic and social development of the Soviet Union for the respective period for all republics, other national and administrative-territorial formations, enterprises, organisations, and institutions. The Plan established in elaborated form the volume indicators for the country as a whole and in summary form for each union republic individually. As

---

[101]   When the legislator places the USSR, the republics, and local soviets on the same level, he is not entirely correct, since in reality local soviets are agencies of power of the respective subject (having in view the territory, region, city, district) and act in its name. A local soviet is not the owner of municipal property to such an extent, nor is the USSR Supreme Soviet the owner of Union property, nor the union republic supreme soviet the owner of republic property.

a result, when working out its own Plan the republic was bound by indicators consolidated in the Plan of the USSR.

This hierarchical structure was inherent to plans confirmed at the lower level. Plans of a union republic were binding upon an autonomous republic within its frontiers, and autonomous republic plans (and in union republics not having autonomous republics, the union republic plans directly) were binding upon its regions, and regional plans were binding upon the cities and districts there, and so on. In confirming the unified State plan for the entire country, the USSR Supreme Soviet effectuated in the name of the State the rights belonging to the State simultaneously as sovereign and as owner. The 1990 USSR Law on Ownership has separated unified State ownership into the ownership of the USSR, the ownership of the union and autonomous republics, and the ownership of other national formations and administrative-territorial entities (the last being called municipal ownership).

The process of dividing the unified State ownership among the aforesaid subjects will require some time.[102] In the meantime, the procedure for planning the national economy has been drastically changed. The 1991 USSR Plan was entitled in draft: "Deepening the Economic Reform and Developing Market Relations."

The respective document adopted by the USSR Supreme Soviet on 12 January 1991[103] contained merely

---

[102]   The Decree of the USSR Supreme Soviet introducing the 1990 Law on Ownership into effect provided that the division of ownership should be completed by 1 July 1991. That deadline has not been met, but the process is underway. Many State enterprises have petitioned for and received permission to transfer from USSR to republic jurisdiction. Some republics are proposing to "nationalise" Union property within their frontiers.

[103]   *Vedomosti SND SSSR* (1991), no. 4, item 70. The Decree was entitled: "On the All-Union Forecast of the Government of the USSR Concerning the Functioning of the Economy in 1991 and on the State Plan for 1991 Regarding the Spheres of Jurisdiction of the USSR."

indicators connected with the activities of enterprises within USSR jurisdiction; that is, those whose property constitutes Union ownership. As regards the republics, the Decree of 12 January 1991 simply incorporated recommendations, such as to seek out material resources in order to increase the production of consumer goods and services, to work out economic measures within the established periods that would ensure in 1991 that the amount of incompleted or delayed construction would be reduced, as well as the "approval of intentions," such as the intentions of the republics to further concentrate financial resources for resolving social problems, raising the standard of living, improving ecological security, and increasing capital investments in the nonproduction sphere in comparison with 1990. Such recommendations can not be regarded as binding upon a republic.

2.   Paragraph two of this Article determines the base points for coordinating the activities of the USSR and the republics. The possibility of such coordination is ensured, *inter alia*, by the fact that in the formative stage the draft plans of respective Union agencies (USSR Ministry of Finances, State Committee of the USSR for Construction and Investment, and others) bring to the information of the Government of each republic the requisite economic information. The information must include data concerning imminent changes in the estimate value of construction and assembly work, the amount of amortisation deductions for full restoration of the asset portion of production funds, information enabling allowing the density of the all-union market to be evaluated, lists of major work being financed with regard to fundamental scientific research, ceilings of State centralised capital investments from the Union budget which are directed to special purposes for building major objects ensuring

production development in key spheres of the economy, and for the construction of individual nature-protection and socio-cultural objects. The respective norm has the aim of assisting republics not only to form their own plans, but also to participate jointly with the USSR in working out a common programme and to determine ways of realising it with regard to the investment activity of the union republic. One such way is the creation of various types of social funds as mentioned in paragraph two of this Article, and also to participate in measures being effectuated by the USSR for the prevention and elimination of the consequences of natural disasters and accidents. Republic laws, amongst them the 1990 RSFSR Law on the formation of budgets of the RSFSR in 1991,[104] allow the transfer of special-purpose financial resources by the republic to the USSR not only to realise the powers delegated to the USSR but also to cover expenditures in the interests of the republics.

3. The list contained in paragraph two of this Article is merely an exemplary one and respectively allows the formation of other funds in order to resolve socio-economic tasks in addition to those mentioned. There exists but one limitation: an agreement on the formation of a fund must not violate the interests of other union republics or lead to the undermining of a unified all-union market.

A nation-wide fund created in 1991, as well as individually in each republic, for stabilising the economy occupies a special place. The all-union fund is to ensure the normal functioning of the economy of the Soviet Union, finance investment, scientific research, and other

---

[104]   Adopted 31 October 1990. *Vedomosti SND SSSR* (1990), no. 22, item 262.

programmes in the interests of the republics, expenditures for conversion, and subventions to individual republics (on subventions, see the Commentary to Article 11, paragraph four). The Edict of the President of the USSR of 29 December 1990[105] determined not only the orientations of use, but also the sources for the creation of the fund (various types of deductions from enterprises and revenues from the realisation of State property).

4.   Paragraph three of this Article corresponds to the second paragraph. Ultimately it has in view joint activity of the Union and the republics. Such activity, including lawmaking, must rest on Union and republic legislation.

5.   The powers of local soviets referred to in paragraph four of this Article are established chiefly by the 1990 USSR Law on the General Principles of Local Self-Government and Local Economy in the USSR.[106] The republics in 1991 began to issue their own laws on local government.[107]

The 1990 USSR Law provides that the competence of agencies of self-government is determined together with the Law itself by other Union and republic acts. The USSR Law gives to the local soviet the right to confirm plans for the territory by proceeding from available material-financial resources, the need to maximally involve local resources and production reserves, and protect the environment. Guarantees of the autonomy of local soviets

[105]   *Vedomosti SND SSSR* (1991), no. 1, item 54.

[106]   *Vedomosti SND SSSR* (1990), no. 16, item 267; no. 44, item 914; transl. in W. E. Butler (ed.), *Basic Documents on the Soviet Legal System* (2d ed., 1991), pp. 127-138.

[107]   The 1991 RSFSR Law on Local Self-Government in the RSFSR appears in *Rossiiskaia Gazeta*, 1 August 1991, pp. 2-6.

are provided, expressed especially in the fact that all questions connected with the creation and transformation of economic and social objects and the use of natural resources on the respective territory may be resolved only with the consent of soviets of people's deputies. The need for the USSR and republics to agree with local soviets questions discussed in this Article is thereby overcome.

One possible form of cooperation is the creation of construction funds common for the republic and local soviet. The local soviet might contribute both budgetary and extrabudgetary assets to such funds. Extrabudgetary funds are obtained by local soviets through economies in expenditure, voluntary contributions and donations of citizens, enterprises, and organisations, revenues from local lotteries and loans, amounts paid in the form of fines by offenders for the irrational use of natural resources, and others. Extrabudgetary assets of local soviets are kept in individual accounts and spent by the possessors of those accounts at their discretion. Local soviets may, in particular, combine the budgetary and extrabudgetary assets which belong to them with the assets of enterprises for the construction, repair, and maintenance on share principles of objects of the social and production infrastructure (clubs, electric power stations, and the like), as well as for implementing nature-protection measures. Such combining of assets by local soviets and enterprises, or for that matter with the USSR or republic, must be on the basis of contracts freely concluded between the parties.

Investment Activity

Article 14: Procedure for Taking Decisions Regarding Union State Investments

1. Decisions relating to Union State investments shall be adopted on the basis of forecasts of the economic and social development of the USSR and schemes for the development and siting of production forces, special purpose scientific-technical and integrated Union programmes, and feasibility studies determining the advisability of such investments.

2. Draft special purpose integrated programmes of Union significance shall be worked out in the procedure determined by the USSR Council of Ministers, with the participation of union republic councils of ministers, interested State agencies, and social organisations and shall be submitted by the USSR Council of Ministers for consideration to the USSR Supreme Soviet.

3. The USSR Supreme Soviet within the State plan for economic and social development of the USSR shall confirm capital investments for the creation of large-scale national economic complexes included on a list of objects of a Union order of the State, as well as amounts of Union State investments.

4. When planning Union investments, the USSR Council of Ministers, with the participation of union republic councils of ministers, shall ensure their

conformity to the amounts of investments needed for the realisation of special-purpose integrated programmes of Union significance and the Union order of the State within the established periods.

5. Appropriations from the Union budget shall be allocated only for the most important construction sites of a Union order of the State and the realisation of all-union programmes.

Within the Union budget shall be allocated a special financial development programme which determines expenditures for the effectuation of investment measures.

Forms for the use of funds of the financial development programme may be either without repayment or on a repayment basis.

6. Joint investing with the participation of Union State investments shall be effectuated in the procedure established by the present Fundamental Principles for the realisation of Union State investments.

1. Special-purpose comprehensive programmes have been used for decades and constituted a major portion of the State plan for social and economic development. The new procedure referred to in point 2 of this Article has not been worked out by the Government of the USSR, which leaves in force that used to draft instructive regulations of the former State Planning Committee of the USSR, abolished in April 1991.[108] Those instructive

regulations provide for separate stages in working out programmes (from drawing up the list of national economic problems subject to inclusion in the programme up to their real incorporation in the respective State plan, the principal requirements for the content of the programme, and others).[109] There is a considerable need to improve the principles for drafting comprehensive special-purpose programmes in order to make them more democratic, as contemplated by the FPInvA.

2. This Article, including point 1, is devoted to instances where the source of investments is exclusively or at least particially the Union budget. It should be borne in mind that the republics will adopt an act having the same or a similar name to regulate investment relations effectuated at the expense of the republic or local budgets.

3. The division of the unified State ownership fund into USSR, republic, and other administrative-territorial entity funds (see Commentary to Article 13) will bring significant modifications of the procedure for drawing up and confirming the budget. Before the 1990 USSR Law on Ownership was adopted, the USSR Supreme Soviet annually confirmed a Law on the State Budget of the USSR which provided for the total amount of revenues for the country and divided them by their basic sources and the total amount of expenditures, singling out the appropriations for financing the national economy,

---

[108] On the former procedures, see *Sovershenstvovanie khoziaistvennogo mekhanizma. Sbornik dokumentov* (1982), pp. 95-102. For the abolition of the State Planning Committee, see Decree No. 176 of the USSR Cabinet of Ministers adopted 13 April 1991. *Pravitel'stvennyi vestnik*, no. 17 (1991), p. 5.

[109] See A. F. Nozdrachev, *Gosudarstvennoe planirovanie i pravovoe regulirovanie. Ekonomika* (1982), pp. 81ff.

socio-cultural measures, defence, and the like. The State Budget of the USSR also indicated the planned amount of revenues and expenditures for the Union budget and individually by the State budgets for each union republic. In turn, the union republic allocated in the State budget the republic budget and especially the budgets of inferior links (autonomous republics, autonomous regions, autonomous national areas, regions). It should be stressed that the union republic was bound by those indicators when confirming its own budget that the USSR Supreme Soviet had confirmed for it.

The principle of the unity of the State budget of the Soviet Union was in its day consolidated in a number of Union and republic acts. Most notable amongst them is the Law on Budget Rights of the USSR and Union Republics,[110] which contains a special section devoted to the State budgets of the union republics. The Law sets out in detail the sources of revenues, the orientation of assets, and other indicators relevant to therepublic budgets. Each union republic adopted analogous acts in development of the USSR Law. An example is the RSFSR Law on the Budget Rights of the RSFSR, Autonomous Republics, and Local Soviets.[111] The substance of republic laws on budget rights was predetermined for the most part of the Union enactment.

These Union and republic budget laws have still not been repealed even though they are obsolete and indeed contrary to laws more recently adopted by the Union and the republics. An example is the 1990 USSR Law on the delimination of powers between the USSR and subjects of the federation,[112] which relegated to the Union competence

---

[110]   Adopted 10 April 1959. *Vedomosti SSSR* (1959), no. 16, item 271.

[111]   Adopted 16 December 1961. *Vedomosti RSFSR* (1961), no. 48, item 679.

[112]   Adopted 26 April 1990. *Vedomosti SND SSSR* (1990), no. 19, item 329; transl. in

the drawing up, confirmation, and execution of the Union budget and the establishment of all-union taxes and charges. In a 1990 USSR Law adopted slightly earlier on the basic principles of economic relations between the USSR and the republics it was provided that the procedure for drawing up, considering, confirming, and executing the Union budget is determined by the USSR Supreme Soviet, whereas those questions relating to the State budget of the republic are determined by the union republic legislator.[113]

Analogous norms operate with respect to local soviets. The 1990 USSR Law on general principles of local self-government provided that local soviets of people's deputies autonomously work out, confirm, and execute the budget of the respective territory in the interests of its populace.[114] The guarantee of autonomy is the norm incorporated in the Law itself: the interference of superior agencies in the process of confirming and executing local budgets is not permitted.

The legislation adopted in 1990 enables one to conclude that the recognition by the 1990 USSR Law on Ownership of a multiplicity of subjects or bearers of the right of ownership to property which previously had merely one owner in the person of the State as such has led to the fact that each subject -- the USSR, union and autonomous republics, other national formations and administrative-territorial entities -- have received exclusive rights to determine the fate of their property, including budget assets. They respectively may now autonomously

W. E. Butler (ed.), *Basic Documents on the Soviet Legal System* (2d ed., 1991), pp. 45-49.

[113]   Adopted 10 April 1990. *Vedomosti SND SSSR* (1990), no. 16, item 270; transl. in W. E. Butler (ed.), *Basic Documents on the Soviet Legal System* (2d ed., 1991), pp. 235-242.

[114]   Adopted 9 April 1990. *Vedomosti SND SSSR* (1990), no. 16, item 267; no. 44, item 914; transl. in W. E. Butler (ed.), *Basic Documents on the Soviet Legal System* (2d ed., 1991), pp. 127-138.

establish from which sources and in what amount they will receive assets in their budgets and how those assets shall be spent.

The said principle was first realised in practice when the budgets were adopted in 1991. The respective USSR Law[115] encompassed merely indicators for the Union budget.[116] Thereafter each republic adopted its own budget, thereby making it possible for the local soviets to autonomously determine the revenues and expenditures of their budgets.

These enactments of the USSR presuppose that the Union budget has its own allocated sources for revenues in the form of all-union taxes and certain other revenues. Individual republics have expressed doubt about this; they suggest that enterprises and citizens domiciled on their territory must pay all taxes to the republic and the republic itself shall decide how much and what to transfer to the Union budget. This approach was reflected in the 1990 RSFSR Law on forming the budgets in the RSFSR for 1991,[117] which provided that only the republic, in order to realise powers delegated by it to the USSR, and also to effectuate expenditures in the interests of the RSFSR, transmits special-purpose financial assets to the Union budget. It is wholly evident that in this event there is a conflict between Union and republic legislation. The view of the last requires careful consideration, for it would undoubtedly weaken the position of the USSR as a sovereign State. Evidently, as in the case of so many other "wars of laws" in the Soviet Union, the final resolution

---

[115]   The USSR Law on the Union Budget for 1991, adopted 12 January 1991. *Vedomosti SND SSSR* (1991), no. 4, item 76.

[116]   The republic budget is only part of the State budget of the republic, for the latter represents the sum total of the republic and all local republic budgets.

[117]   *Vedomosti SND RSFSR* (1990), no. 22, item 262.

will be in the Treaty of the Union. The decision is more a political one than a technical legal solution.

4. Points 1, 2, and 4 of this Article enumerate documents which are to substantiate a positive decision as to whether to allocate funds from the Union budget. Some of these, for example schemes for the development and siting of productive forces, feasibility studies, and others, are known to existing law. But there are new documents mentioned. Thus, when working out the State Plan for 1991 the All-Union Forecast of the Government of the USSR Concerning the Functioning of the Economy of the Country in 1991 was specified for the first time as one of sources; the "intentions of enterprises and republics" were a major component of the forecast. The All-Union Forecast and similar materials were used to draw up the Decree of the USSR Cabinet of Ministers on Organisational Measures Relating to the Working Out of Production Programmes and Forecasts of the Socio-Economic Development of Enterprises, Regions, Republics, and the USSR for 1992 in Conditions of Forming Market Relations.[118]

5. Point 3 of this Article establishes a direct link between the allocation of capital investments according to the State Plan confirmed by the USSR Supreme Soviet and State (Union) orders. The Union order serves as the direct prerequisite for resolving the issue of allocating assets from the Union budget. On State orders, see the Commentary to Article 16.

---

[118]   *Izvestiia*, 17 June 1991, p. 2.

6.   Points 4 and 5 of this Article are concerned with the need to provide assets from the Union budget for investments taking the form of special-purpose programmes of Union significance. The USSR Law on the Union Budget for 1991 singles out appropriations for three special-purpose programmes: eliminating the damage from the Chernobyl atomic power station; restoring the ecological situation and improving living conditions in the Ural area, and taking priority measures with relocating the Crimean Tatars returning to their homeland after having been illegally exiled from the Crimea.

7.   The requirement in points 4 and 5 that investments using Union budget funds are permitted only for special-purpose programmes or Union orders is of great importance. This means that appropriations from the budget are possible only on condition that a competent agency has confirmed the advisability of the investments either by confirming the special-purpose programme or by issuing the order.

8.   Point 5 provides for two forms of using assets to finance development programmes: with or without repayment. Until recently, only one of these was applied -- without repayment. The existing procedure for releasing budget assets exclusively on a without repayment basis was based on the fact that the Soviet State had extensive opportunities to draw profit, once construction was completed, from the newly created or reconstructed enterprise by various means without resorting to demanding the amounts allotted from the budget be returned. In essence the State "fleeced" the enterprise, using various channels for this purpose simultaneously.

Reference is being made here to the fact that the enterprise had to pay to the budget, first, the established interest on the value of basic production funds and normative standards for circulating assets; second, deductions from profit in the established amount; and finally, the residual profit remaining at the end of the year was handed over. It should be added that an enterprise could not dispose of its basic assets (building, installations, etc.): their transfer by one State enterprise to another such enterprise was performed on the basis of a regulation of the superior competent agency. Only with the transfer of State enterprises in their relations with the budget to a taxation basis and endowing them with the right to not only possess and use, but also to dispose of, their basic assets has the need arisen to use budget appropriations which are repayable.

9.   Point 6 of this Article enlarges the operation of the rest of the norms in Section III, introducing into its sphere not only Union, but also investments made jointly with republics.

Article 15: Expert Examination and Confirmation of Union State Investments in Capital Construction

1. Drafts for the construction of objects at the expense of Union State investments shall be subject to obligatory State expert examination, including conformity to requirements of anti-monopoly legislation, the procedure for conducting which shall be established by the USSR Council of Ministers.

2. Expert examination of draft special purpose integrated programmes of Union significance, as well as the most important and large-scale objects of a Union order of the State, shall be effectuated by expert commissions created by decisions of the USSR Council of Ministers, in which shall be included representatives of scientific, social, and other organisations and respective regions; foreign specialists also may be recruited.

3. Designs of special-purpose integrated programmes and the most important and large-scale objects of a Union order of the State shall be submitted for confirmation of the USSR Supreme Soviet together with the opinions of the expert commissions.

4. A Union order of the State for the construction of objects shall be confirmed after

agreement of the siting thereof with the republic and local State agencies in the procedure established by legislation of the USSR and the union and autonomous republics.

1. A design is a legal act, a necessary planning-organisational prerequisite for capital construction. Point 1 of this Article treats designs as something similar to standards since both are subject to confirmation by a competent agency and binding upon the addressees. Just as a standard, a design consolidates the requirements of a technical or technological nature. A comparison with the design enables the quality of the object being built to be evaluated. But there is a material difference between a design and a standard as legal acts. Construction differs from ordinary production in that the ultimate product (a building, installation, etc.) is individual, even unique. Consequently, the design must be individual too. A standard, however, is a complex of rules, requirements, binding in specified domains of activity. Thus a standard is a normative act, whereas a design is a rule for a one-off action. The working out, confirmation, and application of designs is itself subordinate to particular norms, amongst which are standards.

2. A feasibility study and financial feasibility study precedes the preparation of the draft. It determines what precisely is to be built, when the construction is to be completed, and what its cost is to be. Of the two documents the feasibility study is the more elaborate because it is essential for building large-scale and complex enterprises. Both documents, however, have in principle the same purpose and same legal significance: to confirm

the advisability of the investment. For this reason when construction is to be at the expense of budget assets, these documents are the basic source for adopting the decision to make the appropriation. Each is subject to confirmation by the competent agency, determined by the subordination of the customer or investor. Once either is confirmed, it becomes a binding document upon subjects for the investment process: designer, customer or investor, and independent-work contractor or organisation which is to realise the design. The design must conform to the feasibility study or financial feasibility study, and the completed construction of the object must conform to the design.

3. The designing may pass through one or two stages. During the first, the design and working documentation are worked out, and during the second both documents (design and working documentation) are combined in a working design. The legislator here prefers the simpler, second variant. It has accordingly been established that the two-stage designing is essential chiefly in instances when the construction or large-scale or complex industrial complexes is contemplated which presuppose the use of new production technology, new designs of complex technological equipment, complex architectural and construction decisions, or when construction is undertaken under complex conditions. Certain designs need to be coordinated with supervisory and other interested organisations (especially when agreement with State supervision agencies is required). The State Committee of the USSR for Construction and Investment has determined precisely what the sections must contain in the design or working design, depending upon whether they have in view the construction or production objects or housing. For example, for the first

there are sections on technological decisions, organisation of labour of workers and employees, construction decisions, organisation of construction, ensuring environmental protection, and the like. The same framework is provided for working documentation, which must include working drawings, basic requirements for working out construction design documentation, lists of the objects of construction and assembly work, and the like.

The estimate must include the so-called estimate account, composite expenses, local estimates, and others.

4.   Point 1 of this Article calls attention to the need to comply with anti-monopoly legislation. One should bear in mind that throughout the history of the Soviet Union the principle of specialisation has been consistently pursued, which presupposes the concentration of the production of a particular product, service, or work in the smallest number of enterprises. As a result, such enterprises began to occupy a dominant position in a particular region or even nationwide. In a centrally administered economy the negative consequences of this concentration could not culminate because the conclusion of contracts with specific parties, as well as the basic content of the contracts (including quantitative and qualitative indicators), ultimately were predetemined by planning acts binding upon the parties (funds, allocation orders, and the like). The situation has changed, for it has become possible to take certain steps towards the development of market relations, which undoubtedly presuppose the freedom of contract, that is, an autonomous choice of contracting parties, determination of the content of the contract by the parties themselves, including the price of the product, work, or service. Unexpectedly for many, the Soviet Union

is a country with the greatest monopoly of manufacturers of various types of products, work, and services.

The monopoly of manufacturers, and of consumers, means they can dictate their terms to contracting parties. It has become necessary to work out measures directed towards eliminating or at least limiting monopolistic tendencies of individual participants of turnover. It is intended to develop free competition, without which the market economy can not exist and which in and of itself is the most efficient means of combatting monopolistic inclinations. The respective measures were first set out in a Decree of the USSR Council of Ministers on measures relating to demonopolisation of the national economy, adopted 16 August 1990.[119] Some measures are of a general character, whereas others are intended for individual spheres or branches of the national economy. It is provided in particular that enterprises and organisations occupying a dominant market position (those whose share is not less than 70% of the economic turnover of the respective type of product, work, or service) do not have the right to limit or terminate production, refuse to conclude contracts with consumers when they have the real possibility of manufacturing the product, fulfil the work, or render the service. A violation of these requirements[120] entails various consequences unfavourable to the "monopolist." Among those consequences is an instruction to terminate the violations; restoration of the initial position, as well as entering the amounts of unjustified revenues received in the budget, and compensating losses. Depending upon the

---

[119]   *SP SSSR* (1990), no. 24, item 114.

[120]   Specially singled out are such violations as agreements or individual actions of participants of turnover directed towards dividing the market, excluding or limiting the access to the market of other participants of economic turnover, artificially increasing or reducing or maintaining prices for the purposes of receiving an unjustifiably high profit or eliminating competitors, and others.

character of the violation, the respective amounts are recovered for the revenue of the budget or to the benefit of the victim party.

The republics may adopt their own anti-monopoly legislation. The RSFSR on 22 March 1991 did so in the form of the Law on Competition and Limitation of Monopolistic Activity in Goods Markets.[121]

As regards investment activity, the reduction commencing from 1991 of the amounts of centralised budget appropriations should be noted; these must be replaced by funds of investors, the taking of measures to diversify production, creating competitive production entities and back-up enterprises, placing orders for design and construction design work on a competitive basis, and the like. The programme aimed at developing inter-bank competition also should be noted, for therein has been placed a fundamental principle: full equating of the rights of State and commercial banks.

The essence of the requirements laid down in point 1 of this Article is that the realisation of a design should not lead to the creation of yet another monopoly in any branch whatever.

5. The object of State expert examination is a package of documents comprising in aggregate the design or working draft and estimate. When carrying on the expert examination compliance with the design feasibility study and financial feasibility study is taken into account, as well as the requirements established by laws and subordinate acts, including standards, construction norms, and rules. Thus with regard to the construction of

---

[121]   *Ekonomika i zhizn'*, no. 19 (1991), pp. 24-25.

buildings and installations, it is necessary to determine whether the design corresponds to the general plan for the development of the city or other population centre, whether the achievements of science, technology, and progressive experience are realised therein, whether a high technical-economic level has been ensured, the efficiency of capital investments, and others. The use of technological processes and equipment in designs which does not meet the most modern achievements of science and technology is prohibited; however, in practice these requirements are frequently violated.

6. On special purpose comprehensive programmes, see the Commentary to Article 14.

7. On State orders, see the Commentary to Article 16.

8. Points 2, 3, and 4 require expert examination only when the need to effectuate investments arises from special-purpose programmes or was predetermined by the inclusion of a construction site in the most major objects of a Union order (regrettably, the question remains open as to who establishes the degree of importance of the object). As regards both cases, it is provided that the expert examination of large-scale and technically complex designs is to be done by the State Committee of the USSR for Construction and Investment, as renamed in April 1991, and by analogous committees of the union republics and competent agencies of local soviets of people's deputies.

9. Expert examination also is mandatory for investments which must be effectuated from a republic or local budget. The methods of conducting it doubtless will be set out in the republic legislation on investment activity. At present USSR ministries and departments conduct expert examinations with regard to enterprises of Union subordination; republic agencies do so when the construction site has a value of three million rubles or more, and determine the procedure themselves when the construction has a value of less than three million rubles.

Article 16: Procedure for Siting Union Orders of State for Capital Construction

1. One of the forms of the realisation of Union State investments shall be Union orders of the State for capital construction.

2. A Union order of the State in capital construction shall be issued for the creation of production capacities or objects, specifying the periods for their introduction into operation.

3. A Union order of the State shall, as a rule, be placed on a competitive basis. In individual instances the USSR Council of Ministers shall have the right to establish Union orders of the State which are binding upon all State enterprises and organisations who are participants in the investment activity ,taking into account the economic advantage of such orders for enterprises and organisations.

4. The placing of a Union order of the State may, by decision of the USSR Council of Ministers, be entrusted to union republic councils of ministers with their consent and Union agencies of State administration.

5. Any participant of investment activity shall have the right to participate in competitions to receive orders of the State for capital construction.

6. Objects of a Union order of the State shall be accepted for operation in the procedure established by the USSR Council of Ministers.

7. Accounts with independent-work contractors regarding objects of a Union order of the State shall be settled finally after confirmation of the acts of the State Commission.

1. State orders are a relatively new form of planning the national economy which began to be introduced in practice at the end of the 1980s. The procedure for using State orders in the sphere of capital construction has certain distinctive features. The essence is that the plan of social and economic development, hereinafter in the Commentary to this Article the Union plan, includes a list of construction sites at which production capacities are to be created pursuant to a State order. To be sure, these are the most important construction sites financed from the budget (or Union budget) and occasionally from borrowed funds of the enterprise's own assets. State orders are also issued to conduct scientific research and work which "revolutionises social production." The list of objects for which State orders are to be issued is sent to ministries which, in turn, must bring them to the immediate subjects of the investment process: the independent work contractor and the customer.

The order is binding upon State organisations. For cooperative organisations it becomes binding only after the cooperative agreed to accept the order. Joint enterprises with the participation of foreign capital are outside State orders, it being specially stipulated that State orders are not issued to them. Undoubtedly there are reasons to extend the system of State orders also to those participants of turnover, but of course within the regime established for cooperative organisations (having in view that the obligation will thereby arise only when two legal facts are present: a State order and its acceptance by a joint enterprise).

From the State order arises the duty of the independent work contractor-enterprise to conclude a respective contract with the customer specified in the order and to duly perform the obligations arising from the contract.

Specified duties arise from the State order also for the agency which issued it. That agency is obliged to ensure the conclusion by the construction organisation of a contract with the customer specified in the contract. If the customer refuses to conclude the contract, the agency which issued the State order must replace the customer specified therein with another or revoke or change the order. In either situation there are unfavourable consequences for the agency which issued the order (see Commentary to Article 22).

Certain incentives have been provided for organisations which accept an order. The amounts of payments to the budget are reduced within established limits. However, if the addressee of the order does not perform the contractual obligations (violating the conditions of the contract concerning the amount or periods for performing the work or the periods for introducing the production capacities into operation), he is deprived of the respective privilege. Another incentive is that the agency which issued the order is obliged to allot specified quotas of important material resources to the independent-work contractor. The existence of the quota makes it possible for the independent-work contractor to demand from the manufacturer-enterprise of the resources the conclusion of a contract of delivery within the limits of the quota.

State orders all the same reduce the initiative of enterprises: their economic autonomy is materially limited. For this reason State orders are deemed to be a provisional measure for the transition to free market relations. Having regard to this, it has been provided that a State order in the domain of capital construction must not encompass the entire capacity of an enterprise. Within limits strictly established by the Government of the USSR itself they are granted the opportunity to fulfil work above the order. State orders in 1989 were not to exceed more than 90%, and in 1990 75%, of the production capacities of a construction organisation, so that the balance could be used freely with any contracting party.

2. A State order is not always a necessary evil. There are situations when several enterprises have an interest in receiving a State order because for various reasons they are experiencing difficulties in finding contracting parties or in obtaining material resources, and the like. The Government of the USSR has given ministries and departments the right to organise tenders for State orders. The organiser of the tender works out the terms, determines the period for holding it, brings the tender to the notice of potential participants, amongst whom there may be State or cooperative construction

organisations. The offer deemed to be best is the basis for the issuance of a State order to the winner of the tender.

3. The State order, and herein lies its rationale, is the basis for concluding the respective contract. Of all the types of economic contracts in existence for relations formed in the course of effectuating investment activity, three types are of special importance:

- the contract for the fulfilment of design and survey work. This contract, as from 1 January 1992, is to be concluded on the basis of the 1991 FPCivL.[122] In some measure, at least in the early days, such contracts doubtless will continue to be influenced by the 1959 Rules on Contracts for the Fulfilment of Design and Survey Work.[123] Long before perestroika, however, those Rules were obsolete in many respects.

- the contract for the creation or transfer of a scientific-technical product[124] also has become obsolete, although of more recent vintage. Under the 1991 FPCivL it appears to have been subsumed under the Contract on the Fulfilment of Scientific-Research and Experimental Construction Design Work (Article 97).

---

[122]   Article 96. See W. E. Butler (intro. & transl.), *The USSR Fundamental Principles of Civil Legislation* (1991).

[123]   Confirmed 20 February 1959 by the State Committee for Construction, State Planning Committee, and USSR Ministry of Finances. See *Istochniki sovetskogo grazhdanskogo prava* (1961), p. 614. The first confirming agency has been reformed into the State Committee of the USSR for Construction and Investment, and the second was abolished in April 1991.

[124]   Regulated by the Statute on Contracts for the Creation (or Transfer) of a Scientific-Technical Product, confirmed by the State Committee for Science and Technology on 19 November 1987. See *Polnyi khoziaistvennyi raschet i samofinansirovanie. Sbornik documentov* (1988), p. 335ff.

- the independent-work contract for capital construction has traditionally been regulated by numerous enactments adopted at various levels, including the 1961 FPCivL (Articles 67-71), the union republic civil codes, and especially the 1986 Rules on Independent-work Contracts for Capital Construction.[125] The basic provisions as from 1 January 1992 are governed by the 1991 FPCivL (Article 95).

It should be noted that the various normative acts governing the aforesaid contracts are, in principle, revolutionised by the 1991 FPCivL. The latter document to a considerable extent undertakes to transform what previously were centralised, imperative requirements leaving little for the parties to actually negotiate. Additional Union and republic legislation should in the spirit of the market transition elaborate the 1991 FPCivL in the direction of enhancing the economic and legal autonomy of the investors and participants in investment activity.

4. Questions connected with the acceptance and handing over of an object which is completed are regulated by the Decree of the USSR Council of Ministers of 23 January 1981.[126] This Decree is applicable irrespective of how the construction was financed (from the customer's own funds, budget, or bank loan). The Decree requires that the acceptance of objects which are ready must be by a State Acceptance Commission, and determines who appoints the State commission (which, depending upon the significance of the object and its cost, may be the

---

[125]   Confirmed by Decree of the USSR Council of Ministers on 26 December 1986. *SP SSSR* (1987), no. 4, item 19.

[126]   *SP SSSR* (1981), no. 7, item 43.

Government of the USSR, the ministry or department of the customer, or a union republic government), what persons must be on the commission (for objects of production designation this will be, in addition to representatives of the customer and the general independent-work contractor, representatives of the local soviet of people's deputies, sanitary supervision agencies, the general design agency, State fire agencies, technical and labour inspectorates, the financing bank, and the like), who must be the chairman of the commission (usually an executive from the ministry or department which is the customer). Before an object is submitted to the State Acceptance Commission for consideration, a working commission must evaluate whether the object conforms to the design, test equipment, and verify the readiness of the object for normal operation. The working commission does not have the right to accept an object with imperfections or uncompleted elements, and the same is true of the State Acceptance Commission. The Decree specifies which of the participants of investment activity (customer, design or research organisation, independent-work contractor) bears responsibility, and for what. The acceptance is formalised by an act which evaluates the quality of the object. The date of drawing up the acceptance act by the State Commission is simultaneously the date of the introduction of the object into operation.

While the imperative force of the acceptance procedures will decline under the freedom of contract allowed by the 1991 FPCivL, the patterns it incorporates are ones of long-standing which may guide Soviet contractor and customers for some time to come.

5. For many years the settlement of accounts between parties to an independent-work contract for

capital construction and for the performance of design and survey work occurred in instalments on the basis of interim and final documents. This system gradually came to be replaced by another under which payment was made in principle at the end when the enterprise was completed and handed over for operation. In 1990 this last system became in effect the sole scheme, and it assumes that the independent-work contractor covers his current expenses with his own or borrowed assets.

6. The basis for the settlement of accounts remains the acts of the State Acceptance Commission certifying that the object has been accepted into operation. Only those objects which correspond to the design and estimate documentation, both in cost and substance, are to be paid for. However, under the 1991 FPCivL, the parties may agree another procedure for ensuring the construction of and payment for work. (Article 95[2]). A contract price determined by the customer and accepted by the independent-work contractor is deemed to be fixed and unchangeable from the commencement of construction until it is finished.

The distribution of risk in contracts connected with investment activity differs materially from the traditional approach under independent-work contracts. The risk of accidental loss of the subject of a contract usually lies with the independent-work contractor, whereas with respect to contracts connected with investment activity the risk is placed on the customer. Article 95(3) of the 1991 FPCivL provides that in the event of the destruction of or damage to an object of construction as a consequence of insuperable force before the expiry of the period established by the contract for handing over the object, the customer shall be obliged to pay for the value of work performed or of restoration work unless the contract provides otherwise.

Article 17: Procedure for Effectuation of Union State Investments in Securities, Deposits, Movable and Immovable Property, and Other Valuables

1. The amounts of Union State investments for a planned period in securities, deposits, movable and immovable property, and other valuables shall be confirmed by the USSR Supreme Soviet.

2. Investment projects with regard to the aforesaid orientations shall pass through a State expert examination in the procedure established by the USSR Council of Ministers.

1. The list of valuables contained in point 1 of this Article basically coincides with those mentioned in Article 1 (see the Commentary to Article 1).

2. The issuance and subsequent circulation of securities is regulated from 1 January 1992 by the 1991 FPCivL[127] and also by the 1990 Statute on Securities, confirmed by the USSR Council of Ministers, together with special acts devoted to individual types of securities.[128]

---

[127]   Adopted 31 May 1991 and entered into force 1 January 1992. See *Izvestiia*, 25 June 1991, pp. 3-7; transl. in W. E. Butler (intro. & transl.), *The USSR Fundamental Principles of Civil Legislation* (1991).

[128]   The USSR Statute on Securities was confirmed by Decree no. 590 of 19 June 1990. *SP SSSR* (1990), I, no. 15, item 82; transl. in W. E. Butler (ed.), *Basic Documents on the Soviet Legal System* (2d ed., 1991), pp. 345-354.

3. The 1991 FPCivL defines the concept of a security as a "document certifying a property right which may be effectuated only when presenting the original of this document ..." (Article 31). Six types of securities are mentioned: bond, cheque, bill of exchange, stock, bill of lading, and savings certificate. Omitted from this list, but included in the 1990 Statute on Securities, are treasury obligations of the State. In addition to the requirement of presenting the original document, a security also must contain the obligatory requisites provided for by legislation. The absence of those requisites makes the security void.

4. The definitions of each type of security vary somewhat as between the 1991 FPCivL and the 1990 USSR Statute on Securities. According to the FPCivL a stock is a security which certifies the right of its holder to receive part of the profit of a joint-stock society in the form of dividends, to participate in the management of the affairs of the joint-stock society, and to receive part of the property remaining after the liquidation of the joint-stock society. This definition confines the issuance of stock to a joint-stock society, whereas the 1990 USSR Statute on Securities speaks of stock being issued by a joint-stock society or "other enterprise, organisations, commercial bank ..."it would seem the latter is possible only if those entities are organised as joint-stock societies.

The distinguishing features of a stock, as defined in the 1990 USSR Statute on Securities, are that it normally has no specified period of circulation; it certifies that assets have been contributed for the purpose of developing the enterprise; it gives the right to receive dividends; it may be bearer or inscribed; it is always indivisible; it is issued in the amount of the charter fund (additional stocks may be issued only after the others have been fully paid up); and the stock is secured by all of the property of the joint-stock society.

In addition to the differences between the 1991 FPCivL and the 1990 USSR Statute on Securities, republic legislation also has introduced innovations. The Statute on Joint-Stock Societies confirmed by Decree of the RSFSR Council of Ministers on 25 December 1990, for example, allows only inscribed stocks to be issued (on conflicts between Union and republic legislation, see the Commentary to Article 18).

5. A bond, according to the 1991 FPCivL, is a security certifying the right of its holder to receive from the person who issued the bond within the period provided thereby the par value of the bond or other equivalent property, plus the amount of interest fixed therein on the par value, or other property rights. There are State and local bonds, as well as bonds issued by joint-stock societies or other enterprises. They may be bearer or inscribed and of free or limited circulation, and interest-bearing or not. Non-interest bearing bonds are usually "special purpose loans" which give the purchaser the right to acquire a particular good after a specified period (usually an automobile). The agency which issues State or local bonds (Government of the USSR or republic, or local soviet of people's deputies) usually fixes special conditions. Those organisations bear responsibility for the loans, according to the 1990 USSR Statute on Securities, although in reality with respect to all actions connected with the issuance of bonds such agencies act in the name of the USSR or the respective republic or other administrative-territorial or national formation. They are liable for the loans with their respective budget assets.

Special norms on bonds are to be found in RSFSR legislation on joint-stock societies and limited responsibility partnerships.

6. As regards savings certificates, the 1991 FPCivL and the 1990 USSR Statute on Securities differ in their respective definitions. The FPCivL define such a certificate as being issued by a bank and concerning the deposit of cash assets which the depositor has the right to receive when the certificate expires together with the interest thereon. The 1990 USSR Statute on Securities also refers to the right of a "credit institution" to issue such certificates. The certificates may be bearer or inscribed and may be issued for a specified period or not.

7. A State treasury obligation is defined only in the 1990 USSR Statute on Securities. It is similar to a savings certificate in that it confirms the right of the holder (only citizens may be holders) to receive back the cash assets contributed by them to the State budget and to receive a fixed income through the period that they hold the treasury obligation.Treasury obligations may be long-term (5-25 years), medium term (1-5 years), or short term (3, 6, and 12 months). This type of security is regulated in detail by the Conditions for the Issuance of State Treasury Obligations of the USSR, confirmed by the USSR Council of Ministers.[129]

---

[129]   The Conditions were confirmed on 29 December 1989 by Decree No. 1178 and amended 7 July 1990 by Decree No. 653. The latter appears in *SP SSSR* (1990), no. 16, item 89. Also relevant is Decree No. 1119 of the USSR Council of Ministers, adopted 21 December 1989, authorising USSR Savings Bank to freely sell State interest-free special-purpose loan bonds.

8. The bill of exchange is a security which certifies the unconditional obligation of the drawer or other payer specified to pay upon the period provided for in the bill of exchange a specified amount to the drawee. This type of security is regulated in detail in a Decree of the Central Executive Committee and Council of People's Commissars of the USSR adopted 7 August 1937.[130] This Decree was adopted to give effect to the USSR accession to the 1930 Convention providing a Uniform Law for Bills of Exchange and Promissory Notes, opened for signature at Geneva.[131] However, it should be borne in mind that the bill of exchange in the Soviet Union was used extensively only in the 1920s, although it has begun to appear again under perestroika. This is because the credit reform carried out on the basis of a Decree of the Central Executive Committee and Council of People's Commissars of the USSR of 3 January 1930 prohibited organisations from engaging in commercial credits; direct bank credits became accordingly the sole form.[132] The prerequisites for using bills of exchange between Soviet enterprises thus disappeared. Taking into account that citizens in those days could no longer carry on entrepreneurial activities, the bill of exchange remained to be used only in foreign trade.

The 1987 USSR Law on the State Enterprise, repealed on 7 March 1991, in authorising State enterprises to "transfer ... cash resources to other enterprises and organisations fulfilling work and services for the enterprise,"[133] opened the door for using commercial credit

---

[130]   *SZ SSSR* (1937), no. 52, item 221.

[131]   Entered into force 1 January 1934. See M. O. Hudson (ed.), *International Legislation* (1936), V, pp. 516-549.

[132]   *SZ SSSR* (1930), no. 8, item 98.

[133]   *Vedomosti SSSR* (1987), no. 26, item 385; *Vedomosti SND SSSR* (1989), no. 9,

and the deferral of payment by consumers for the product, work, or services. Again the prerequisites for using the bill of exchange in domestic turnover were created.

9. The 1991 FPCivL also defines the cheque (Article 34) and the bill of lading (Article 37) as securities.

10. The FPInvA is one of the first laws to use the terms "movable" and "immovable" property. It thereby reinstates the demarcation repealed when the 1922 RSFSR Civil Code was adopted.[134] The absence of the term "immovable property" caused certain difficulties, especially when the term was used in international treaties of the USSR.

11. A special procedure for investing in securities by using budget assets, referred to in point 2 of this Article, still has not been introduced into legislation.

---

item 214. Repealed per *Vedomosti SND SSSR* (1991),no. 12,item 325.

[134]   The Note to Article 21 of the 1922 RSFSR Civil Code provided: "With the abolition of private ownership in land, the division of property into movable and immovable has been eliminated."

Article 18: Activity Regarding the Effectuation of Republic and Municipal State Investments

Republic and municipal State investing shall be effectuated in accordance with the present FPInvA and legislation of the union and autonomous republics.

1. This Article confines itself to indicating that investment activity may be regulated by Union and republic legislation, leaving open the issue as to who has the right to adopt respective acts and when. The 1990 USSR Law on the demarcation of powers between the USSR and republics of the federation determined the exclusive competence of the USSR (therein lies the establishment of the system of State banks of the USSR, the power to levy all-union taxes and charges, and others), as well as questions which are within the joint jurisdiction of the USSR and republics: determining a common finance and credit policy and the basic principles of price formation, the establishment of Fundamental Principles of civil legislation and certain other branches of legislation, the legal foundations which ensure the functioning of the all-union market and the protection thereof in the interests of the republics, and others.[135]

The 1990 USSR Law on the basic principles of economic relations between the USSR and the republics demarcates the competence of the USSR and the republics in a special domain.[136] The Law relegated to USSR

---

[135]   *Vedomosti SND SSSR* (1990), no. 19, item 329; transl. in W. E. Butler (ed.), *Basic Documents on the Soviet Legal System* (2d ed., 1991), pp. 45-49.

[136]   Adopted 10 April 1990. *Vedomosti SND SSSR* (1990), no. 16, item 270; transl. in W. E. Butler (ed.), *Basic Documents on the Soviet Legal System* (2d ed., 1991), pp. 235-242.

jurisdiction the confirmation of all-union standards, the formation of all-union funds, the establishment of general norms and rules for the protection of the environment and natural resources, coordination of republic activities relating to investment and amortisation policies, and the like. Within the competence of the republics is the issue of the possession, use, and disposition of land and other natural resources in their interests and the interests of the USSR, the regulation of investment activity and conditions of construction on the territory of the republic, the regulation of prices by proceeding from the all-union price policy formation, the establishment of ecological security norms, the determination of ceilings and normative standards for nature use, the prohibition of activities of specified enterprises and organisations, and others. It is further provided that the republics are to legislatively establish on their territory and within the limits of their competence a procedure uniform for all investors for the acquisition of property and making of capital investments. Republic legislation must guarantee investors a choice of independent-work contract organisations and the return of investments made and repatriation of revenues received. (see Article 4[5] of the said Law).

Finally, there is a list of questions relegated to USSR competence which may become key ones under the Treaty of the Union and are contained in the Fundamental Orientations for the Stabilisation of the National Economy and Transition to the Market Economy. One of the central ideas of this document is that the "republics shall effectuate the legislative regulation of the possession, use, and disposition of all the national wealth located on their territories, which shall form the material foundation of their State sovereignty." Union ownership shall respectively be regarded as the "joint ownership of all republics." The provisions cited are addressed to Union and republic agencies which are competent to create legal norms. Law enforcement agencies are another matter: for direct participants of turnover, courts, arbitrazh courts, and arbitration courts, it is vital to determine the limits of the operation of legal norms adopted at the Union and republic levels. Virtually everything comes down to answering the question of which norms should guide them in the event of a conflict between Union and republic rules. The problem is especially acute when divergencies amongst them are considerable.

Article 74 of the USSR Constitution provides that "Laws of the USSR shall have the same force on the territory of all union republics. In the event of a divergence between a union republic law and an all-union law, the law of the USSR shall prevail."[137] A similar position is taken by a later enactment, the USSR Law of 24 October 1990 on ensuring the operation of laws and other acts of legislation of the USSR.[138] It proceeds from the absolute priority of Union laws, edicts of the President of the USSR, and other acts issued within the limits of his powers, and also makes provision for a mechanism ensuring that priority.

The approach to joint competence is more cautious. The Law of 26 April 1990 provided that when a particular question relegated to the sphere of joint jurisdiction of the USSR and union republics has not been decided by legislation of the USSR, a union republic has the right to autonomously effectuate the egal regulation of relations in the respective domain.[139] A possible conflict between union

---

[137]   Transl. in W. E. Butler (ed.), *Basic Documents on the Soviet Legal System* (2d ed., 1991), p. 17.

[138]   *Vedomosti SND SSSR* (1990), no. 44, item 918.

[139]   Transl. in W. E. Butler (ed.), *Basic Documents on the Soviet Legal System* (2d ed., 1991), pp. 45-49.

and republic acts with regard to questions within their joint competence is to be decided as follows: the act issued by union agencies is deemed to be in force.

There are no differences of principle between the USSR Constitution and the provisions of the Law of 26 April 1990. Just as Article 74 of the USSR Constitution, the said Law in no way limits the lawmaking powers of the USSR. However, a number of republics have adopted enactments providing in one form or another for the priority of republic laws vis-a-vis laws of the USSR. Declarations on State sovereignty of individual republics (Ukraine, Turkmenistan, and others) stress the supremacy on their territories of the constitution and laws of the republics themselves, thereby deeming republic law to be higher than Union law. The operation of acts of the USSR contrary to sovereign rights of the republic is suspended by the highest agencies of State power and administration of the republic. And the principle of joint competence between the USSR and republic is completely rejected, as is the right of the republic to participate in effectuating the powers voluntarily transferred to the jurisdiction of the USSR.

2.   The position of the RSFSR is of special interest. The RSFSR adopted on 24 October 1990 a Law on the Operation of Acts of Agencies of the USSR on the Territory of the RSFSR[140] It provided that laws and other acts of the highest agencies of State power of the USSR, edicts of the President of the USSR, acts of the USSR Council of Ministers and ministries and departments of the USSR operate directly within the limits of the powers which the RSFSR has transferred to the USSR. In other

---

[140]   See *Sbornik zakonodatel'nykh aktov RSFSR o gosudarstvennom suverenitete, soiuznom dogovore i referendume* (1991), pp. 16-17.

instances for a law of the USSR or act of the President of the USSR to extend to the territory of the RSFSR its ratification is essential, and for other acts the confirmation of the respective agency of the Russian Federation is mandatory.

In all justness it should be noted that the basic provisions of the RSFSR law are closer to the USSR Constitution and other laws of the USSR since they allow the priority of republic legislation only with regard to questions which are outside the powers of the USSR transferred by the republic and only on condition that ratification or confirmation of the Union act by the republic is lacking. The 1990 USSR Law works from the priority of Union laws, Edicts of the President of the USSR, and other acts issued within their powers.

3.   A vast range of opinion has emerged with regard to resolving possible conflicts between Union and republic laws.[141] There are roughly three views. The first is that Union acts possess in all instances priority with respect to republic acts. The second is that Union acts operate on the territory of a republic only on condition that the republic has confirmed its will that this should happen by way of ratification. Third, the exclusive competence of the USSR is recognised with regard to questions whose resolution has been transferred to it by the republic, and with the framework of joint competence the priority of republic norms, except instances when a Union act has been issued to protect the interests of other union republics or the State as a whole (especially a presumption must exist in favour of the priority of Union acts regarding questions connected

---

[141]   See *Pravovye problemy reglamentatsii natsional'nykh otnoshenii v SSSR* (1989); *Pravovye problemy ekonomicheskoi reformy v SSSR* (1990); and "Slyshat' drug druga," *Kommunist,* no. 6 (1989), pp. 62-81.

with ensuring the functioning of a single market for the Soviet Union), is recognised.

Taking into account the principled significance of the respective problem, there is no doubt that its resolution on a more general level lies in demarcating the competence of the USSR and the republics in the Treaty of the Union which is to replace that of 30 December 1922 or in the series of new Union and republic constitutions adopted on the basis of the Treaty. In this connection it should be noted that the USSR Law of 24 October 1990 on the priority of Union laws expressly provides that the priority of Union acts remains only until the adoption of the Treaty of the Union.

4. It is unlikely that Article 74 of the 1977 USSR Constitution is appropriate for the new relations between the Union and the republics. More suitable would be a triad approach defining: (1) the exclusive competence of the USSR; (2) the joint competence of the USSR and republics; and (3) the competence of the republic. Bearing in mind that the sovereignty of the USSR and its right based thereon to issue generally binding acts rests on the expression of will of the republics themselves, the following two circumstances should be taken into account: first, the demarcation of the competence of the USSR and republics may not be determined by the Union legislator since the source of his competence is the rights delegated to him by those who created the Union and in doing so voluntarily limited their sovereignty: the republics. Consequently, the reasons for issuing acts concerning the demarcation of the competence of the Union and the republics will disappear at the Union level. Second, the exclusive competence of the USSR and joint competence of the USSR and republics must be defined exhaustively.

Accordingly, a union republic must have the right to issue norms enjoying priority with regard to all questions except those which fall into the exclusive competence of the USSR or joint competence of the USSR and republic. In the event of a conflict of Union and republic acts regarding questions relegated to the exclusive competence of the USSR, the Union norms have such priority absolutely. The difficulties arise only with respect to joint competence. It is evident that Union acts in this case may enjoy priority only within strictly determined limits. The search for criteria to define these will be a serious problem for the future legislator.

Article 19: Price-Formation in Investment Activity

The value of products (or work, services) in the process of investment activity shall be determined according to contract prices, including according to the results of competitions (or auctions), and in the instances provided for by legislative acts of the USSR and the union and autonomous republics, according to State prices.

A contract price in construction shall be determined by using State estimate norms and prices as recommendatory.

1. Until recently, only prices confirmed by the competent State agency (usually the former State Committee for Prices)[142] could be used in relations between a customer and an independent-work contractor, a customer and he who performs design and survey work, or work relating to the creation or transfer of scientific-technical products. Those prices had to be fixed in the estimate of the design organisation, which then followed them in its accounts with the party to the contract to perform such work. From the mid-1980s, as part of expanding the economic initiative of enterprises, prices agreed by the parties began to become possible. State estimate norms and prices became optional for the parties. The necessary legal foundation for using contract prices in

---

[142]   The State Committee for Prices was abolished by Decree No. 176 of the USSR Cabinet of Ministers, adopted 13 April 1991. Its functions relating to inspection control over prices were transferred to the USSR Ministry of Finances, and questions relating to the effectuation of price policy, to the USSR Ministry of the Economy and Forecasting. See *Pravitel'stvennyi vestnik*, no. 17 (1991), p. 5.

the national economy as a whole, and especially when effectuating investment activity, were laid down in the 1987 Law on the State Enterprise, repealed in 1991.[143]

It provided that an enterprise realises its products, work, or services at prices or tariffs established either centrally, or by contracts with the consumer, or autonomously. Republic legislation went even further in that direction. The 1990 RSFSR Law on Enterprises and Entrepreneurial Activity expressly consolidated the presumption in favour of contract prices and prices established by the enterprise or entrepreneur itself.[144] It acknowledged that State prices might be used only in the instances provided by republic legislation. One such instance is directly linked with anti-monopoly measures: the State must regulate prices for a product, work, or services of enterprises who occupy a dominant market position.

2. The State Committee of the USSR for Construction and Investments, as renamed in April 1991, issued normative acts establishing the procedure for determining contract prices in its guise as the State Construction Committee of the USSR. The parties were at liberty to take account of those requirements at their own risk. Those acts deserve attention for how they single out individual elements of a contract price, for their recommendations as to how to calculate such a price, and for their requirement that a contract must be taken into account when drawing up design and estimate documentation, beginning with the feasibility study. Given the importance of prices for all participants in the

[143]   *Vedomosti SSSR* (1987), no. 26, item 395; *Vedomosti SND SSSR* (1989), no. 9, item 214. Repealed 7 March 1991: *Vedomosti SND SSSR* (1991), no. 12, item 325.

[144]   Adopted 25 December 1990. *Vedomosti SND RSFSR* (1990), no. 30, item 418.

investment process, it is recommended that everyone be involved in agreeing prices, including the general design organisation and subindependent-work contractors, as well as the customer and general independent-work contractor. The price agreed by the parties remains unchanged for all participants of the investment process throughout the duration of the contract. It is further stipulated that when an independent-work contractor works out and realises proposals to improve design decisions, the previously established price continues to apply to accounts between the contracting parties. Thus, the advantage obtained from the respective modification remains with the independent-work contractor.

Section IV: Guarantees of Rights and Protection of Investments

Investment Activity

Article 20: Guarantees of Rights of Subjects of Investment Activity

1. The State shall guarantee the stability of the rights of subjects of investment activity. In instances of the adoption of acts of legislation whose provisions limit the rights of subjects of investment activity, the respective provisions of such acts may not be introduced into effect earlier than a year from the moment of their publication.

2. In the event of the adoption by State agencies of acts which violate the rights of investors and participants of investment activity, the losses, including lost advantage, caused to subjects of investment activity as a result of the adoption of the said acts, shall be compensated by that agency by decision of a court or arbitral tribunal. In the event the assets of that State agency are insufficient, the damage shall be compensated respectively by the USSR or the union or autonomous republic or the local soviet of people's deputies whose agency adopted the act which violated the rights of investors and participants of investment activity.

State agencies and their officials shall not have the right to interfere in the activity of subjects of investment activity, except for instances when such interference is permitted by legislation and is effectuated within the limits of the competence of such agencies and officials.

No one shall have the right to limit the rights of investors in choice of objects of investment, except for instances provided for by the present Fundamental Principles.

3. The termination or suspension of investment activity shall be by decision of:

investors, whereupon the investors shall compensate losses to participants of investment activity;

an empowered State agency.

The decision of a State agency concerning the termination or suspension of investment activity may be adopted by reason of:

an announcement in the procedure established by law of an investor to be bankrupt by virtue of insolvency;

natural disasters and other instances having the effect of insuperable force;

the introduction of an extraordinary situation;

if in the process of investment activity it is elicited that its continuation will lead to a violation of sanitary-hygienic, ecological, and other norms established by legislation or the rights and interests of citizens protected by law, juridical persons, and the State. The procedure for compensation of damage to participants of investment activities in this event shall be determined by legislation of the USSR and the union and autonomous republics.

1. Legislative "acts" here should be understood to mean Union and republic laws, decrees of the USSR Cabinet of Ministers and governments of the union and autonomous republics, departmental and ministerial acts, and the acts of local soviets of people's deputies. For the consequences specified in this Article to ensue there is no need to deem the respective acts to be unlawful. On the contrary, it is understood that they have been issued within the competence of the USSR, republic, or local soviet. Otherwise the normative acts would simply have no legal force for the law enforcement agencies. Normative acts of the USSR, if they are contrary to the sovereignty of a union republic, may be disputed in the USSR Supreme Soviet after having obtained in advance the opinion of the USSR Constitutional Supervision Committee, to be abolished under the next USSR Constitution in favour of the Constitutional Court of the USSR. Acts of autonomous republics and local soviets may be disputed in the procedure provided for by the union republics.

2. Since in point one of this Article no special limitations have been made, one should understand the "subjects of investment activity" to be all those who are contemplated in Article 4 (see Commentary thereto); that is, both investors (those who effectuate investments) and participants (those who ensure investments as "executors of orders or on the basis of a commission of an investor").

3. By "limitation of rights" should be understood the creation of the physical, legal, and under certain conditions, also the economic impossibility of the subjects of investment activity to effectuate the rights which belong

to them as a consequence of the issuance of a new normative act.

4. By "violation of rights" should be understood both rights to a thing and rights of obligations. In the first instance reference is made to the right of ownership or rights of State organisations which derive therefrom,[145] whereas in the second it is the rights of an investor with respect to a participant or of a participant with respect to an investor consolidated in a contract concluded between them (having in view an independent-work contract for capital construction, contract for the fulfilment of design work, and the like).

5. It follows from point 1 of this Article that the conditions of a contract of an investor with a participant of investment activity may provide for the preservation of the operation of the contract after the adoption of a new act for a greater or lesser period in comparison with the twelve-month limit.

From the practical standpoint, point 1 of this Article has a negative dimension. Reference to it may be made by a debtor in his objections against the demands of a creditor based on the new legislation. Presumably the objection must be that twelve months had not elapsed since the adoption of the new law or other period provided for in the contract.

---

[145] That is, State enterprises and budget institutions whose property belonging to the State by right of ownership has been transferred to them in possession, use, and disposition. The 1990 USSR Law on Ownership calls the respective right of State enterprises the "right of full economic jurisdiction" and the right of budget organisations, the "right of operative management." See M. I. Braginskii, W. E. Butler, and A. A. Rubanov (commentary), *The Law on Ownership in the USSR* (1991); and W. E. Butler (intro. & transl.), *The USSR Fundamental Principles of Civil Legislation* (1991).

6. Together with the guarantees provided for by the present FPInvA, an investor may when the appropriate conditions exist use the guarantees provided in a number of other acts. Thus, in a situation when a newly adopted law materially limits the rights of an investor as an owner, Article 31 of the 1990 USSR Law on Ownership applies.[146] This Article ensures broader protection to a victim since the owner is given the possibility in the case where a new law simultaneously terminates the right of ownership belonging to the victim to demand compensation for losses. This demand is addressed by the owner to the USSR or republic, depending upon who adopted the respective law. There is reason here to point to a specific feature of the FPInvA and its relationship with the 1990 USSR Law on Ownership and, indeed, the 1990 RSFSR Law on Ownership. The specific feature is that the consequences provided for by those laws may not compete since the investor's right to compensation of losses arises only after the expiry of the twelve-month period or other period provided by the contract calculated from the moment when the new law is adopted.

7. Point 2 differs from point 1 of this Article in that the former speaks, first, of the consequences of the issuance of an *administrative* act, that is, a specific act of one-off operation (an example is a prescription directed towards an investor expressly or a participant concerning the termination of the investment activity being effectuated by him), and second, about the issuance of an *illegal* act. The last follows directly from the reference to the fact that it has in view the adoption by a State agency of acts which "violate rights."

---

[146]   See M. I. Braginskii, W. E. Butler, and A. A. Rubanov (commentary), *The Law on Ownership in the USSR* (1991), pp. 283-288.

8.   Point 2 of this Article provides for a special case of the more general rule incorporated in Article 89 of the 1961 FPCivL,[147] which is devoted to the delictual responsibility of State institutions for harm caused by the actions of State and social organisations and officials in the domain of administrative management and thereby encompasses the situation set out in this point of the FPInvA. As from 1 January 1992, Article 89 is superseded by Article 127 of the 1991 FPCivL.[148] Whereas Article 89 in the 1961 FPCivL distinguished between whether it was a citizen or a juridical person who was the victim of harm caused in the domain of administrative management, Article 127 of the 1991 FPCivL eliminates that distinction. Responsibility ensues on the general grounds unless provided otherwise by legislative acts. Juridical persons in this event would encompass any juridical persons participating in civil turnover: Soviet, joint, and foreign.

Beginning with the early years of Soviet power and until quite recently three laws were in force with regard to the responsibility of agencies of administration towards organisations. These were enacted in the 1920s and provided responsibility for (1) illegal confiscation; (2) interference in the activity of cooperative organisations; and (3) the actions of a maritime pilot. The first two were not applied in practice even though the basis for doing so arose frequently. Suffice it to point to the well-known "corn era" when at the initiative of N. S. Khrushchev the central and local agencies forced collective farms to sow corn even in those areas where for climatic reasons it could not grow. Apparently not a single demand for the

---

[147]   Transl. in W. E. Butler (comp. & transl.), *The Soviet Legal System: Legislation and Documentation* (1978), pp. 418-419.

[148]   See W. E. Butler (ed.), *The USSR Fundamental Principles of Civil Legislation* (1991).

compensation for losses was made in connection with the forced sowing of corn.

Only recently have acts been adopted which in aggregate create a broad legal basis for redress when harm is caused to organisations. The first of these was the 1987 USSR Law on the State Enterprises, which provided that losses caused to an enterprise as a result of fulfilling instructions of a superior agency that violated the rights of the enterprise or as a result of the superior agency improperly carrying out its duties with respect to the enterprise were subject to compensation by that agency.[149]

An analogous norm appeared in the 1988 USSR Law on cooperative societies in the USSR.[150] Particularly to be noted is the 1990 USSR Law on Ownership, which together with the 1990 RSFSR Law of the same name, granted the right to demand compensation of losses caused by agencies of power and administration to any owners, and thereby to any investors, including Soviet State, cooperative, and social organisations, joint enterprises with the participation of foreign capital, as well as foreign owners carrying on economic, including investment, activities in the USSR.[151]

The line was further narrowed in the 1991 FPCivL, which provides expressly that harm caused to a citizen or to a juridical person by the illegal actions of State agencies, as well as by officials when performing their

---

[149]   Adopted 30 June 1987. *Vedomosti SSSR* (1987), no. 26, item 385; *Vedomosti SND SSSR* (1989), no. 9, item 214. Repealed 7 March 1991. See *Vedomosti SND SSSR* (1991), no. 12, item 325.

[150]   Adopted 26 May 1988. *Vedomosti SSSR* (1988), no. 22, item 355; *Vedomosti SND SSSR* (1989), no. 19, item 350; (1990), no. 26, item 489; transl. as amended in W. E. Butler (ed.), *Basic Documents on the Soviet Legal System* (2d ed., 1991), pp. 355-402.

[151]   See M. I. Braginskii, W. E. Butler, and A. A. Rubanov (commentary), *The Law on Ownership in the USSR* (1991), pp. 283-288.

duties in the domain of administrative management, is to be compensated on the general grounds unless provided otherwise by legislative acts (Article127).[152]

9. By virtue of Articles 127 and 126 of the 1991 FPCivL together (the equivalent of Articles 89 and 88 of the 1961 FPCivL), four conditions must be satisfied for delictual responsibility to arise:

- there must be property damage in the form of losses to the victim. According to Soviet civil legislation, losses are subject to compensation in full. Of the two types of losses, direct and indirect, only the first are compensated, but on the other hand there is no distinction drawn between "foreseeable" and "unforeseeable" losses since both are subject to compensation. The full amount of losses presupposes expenses incurred by the creditor, the loss of or damage to his property, and the recovery of revenues not received by the creditor which he would have received if the obligation had been performed by the debtor. Soviet civil law thus returns to the classical Roman-law formula: unlawfulness or illegality of actions (reflected in the expression "violates the rights" of the victim); causal link (the issuance of an act is the cause, and losses arise as a consequence thereof); fault of the tortfeasor (there being different forms of fault (intent or negligence) and degrees of fault (gross or simple negligence) does not influence the amount of losses subject to compensation).

It follows from the above that either an investor or a participant of investment activity may be a victim, in which case he must prove the existence of the first three factors since the law presumes the fault of the tortfeasor, in

---

[152]   See W. E. Butler (intro. & transl.), *The USSR Fundamental Principles of Civil Legislation* (1991).

this case an agency which has issued the act. The last must prove the absence in his actions of intent or negligence in order to be relieved of responsibility by demonstrating that the act was issued within its competence or within the framework of legislation in force.

10. The agency which issued the act is directly responsible to the victim investor or participant in investment activity. The subsidiary responsibility provided for in this Article for the USSR or republic or local soviet of people's deputies is to be explained by the fact that a State institution or organisation on the State budget is called upon to be liable. Pursuant to Article 26(3) of the 1990 USSR Law on Ownership, if a State institution or organisation lacks assets, responsibility for its obligation is borne by the owner of the property. Here the Article takes into account that the property of a Union agency is the ownership of the USSR, and so on down the administrative hierarchy.[153]

11. There exists yet another consequence of the issuance of an illegal administrative act. The victim has the right to apply to a court or arbitrazh court with a demand to deem the act of the agency of power or administration to be void, which means that no legal consequences would arise from the act. That norm has been consolidated in a number of special laws and applies to an investor or participant who falls under their scope. Such a right, for example, exists when the powers of a citizen to possess, use, and dispose of his property are violated,[154] as well as

---

[153]   See M. I. Braginskii, W. E. Butler, and A. A. Rubanov (commentary), *The Law on Ownership in the USSR* (1991), pp. 237-239.

[154]   See Article 34, 1990 USSR Law on Ownership; Article 32, RSFSR Law on

any organisation irrespective of whether it is held in personal, collective, or State ownership.[155]

12. Paragraph two of point 2 of this Article reproduces with slight alterations the provisions of Article 30(2) of the 1987 USSR Law on the State Enterprise, which was repealed on 7 March 1991. The most common forms of interference are likely to be State inspectorates (fire, gas, electric power, sanitary, and others).

13. Paragraph three of point 2 of this Article is built on the principle that everything is permitted unless expressly prohibited. Prohibitions against certain objects of investment activity are set out in Article 3 of the FPInvA (see the Commentary to Article 3).

14. The termination or suspension of investment activity as regards relations between an investor and participants would mean the dissolution or modification of the contract binding them. Under the administrative-command system Soviet law did know examples of where a unilateral repudiation of the performance of an obligation or a unilateral change of the conditions of a contract were allowed pursuant to Soviet legislation. These exceptions seem to be what point 3 of this Article has in view.

The 1991 FPCivL introduces a market approach to this question which in principle seems to override the

Ownership. Both appear in M. I. Braginskii, W. E. Butler, and A. A. Rubanov (commentary), *The Law on Ownership in the USSR* (1991), pp. 299-305, 370.

[155]   See Article 6, 1991 USSR Law on Entrepreneurship of Citizens in the USSR. Transl. in M. I. Braginskii, W. E. Butler, and A. A. Rubanov (commentary), *The Law on Ownership in the USSR* (1991), p. 382.

provisions of union republic civil codes that would allow unilateral repudiation under certain circumstances. The examples flow mostly from the construction industry, where the Rules on independent-work contracts for capital construction allowed construction to be suspended or terminated and the contract dissolved under designated circumstances. Given that the Rules were issued by bodies now extinct and that they are inconsistent with the 1991 FPCivL, their status is doubtful. Sometimes, however, governmental acts also serve as the basis for dissolution of a construction contract.[156]

15. Insolvency is treated in various legislative acts and is the subject of a separate 1991 USSR Law on bankruptcy. Soviet legislation has, until the 1991 Law, left the procedure for deeming an organisation to be insolvent obscure. To some extent this was the result of poor drafting. The possibility of deeming an organisation to be insolvent was first provided for in a Decree of 21 August 1954 "On the Role and Tasks of the State Bank of the USSR."[157] The USSR State Bank and the Construction Bank of the USSR were given that right. Several years later insolvency was declared to be inadmissible as a sanction to be applied to enterprises and organisations.[158]

The reinstatement of insolvency was proclaimed in several enactments, including the 1987 USSR Law on the

---

[156]   See the Decree of the USSR Council of Ministers of 21 June 1989 "On the Suspension of the Installation and Deferral of the Commencement of Construction of a Number of Large-Scale Expensive Construction Sites and Objects." *SP SSSR* (1989), no. 26, item 95.

[157]   See *Istochniki sovetskogo grazhdanskogo prava* (1960), p. 751.

[158]   See the Decree of the USSR Council of Ministers, 3 April 1967 "On Measures Relating to the Further Improvement of Credits and Accounts in the National Economy and Enhancing the Role of Credit in Stimulating Production." *SP SSSR* (1967), no. 10, item 56.

State Enterprise (repealed on 7 March 1991). The 1990 USSR Law on Banks and Bank Activities authorised banks to deem insolvent juridical persons-borrowers who did not fulfil their obligation to repay credits in a timely way; in this event at the proposal of the bank the superior agency (for a partnership, its participants) appoints the administration, to which operative management is transferred by the delinquent borrower, if the juridical person is reorganised.[159] The 1990 RSFSR Law on Enterprises and Entrepreneurial Activity, however, relegated the declaration of insolvency to the exclusive competence of a court, justifying this approach on the grounds that the enterprise concerned has not fulfilled its obligations either to the bank or to other creditors.[160] Now that a substantial number of commercial banks are operating together with the USSR State Bank and based on various forms of ownership, but not possessing as does the USSR State Bank any administrative functions, the judicial procedure for declaring an enterprise to be insolvent would seem to be the preferred solution.

The expression "bankruptcy" first appeared, after its use in the 1920s, again in the 1990 USSR Law on Enterprises.[161] This Law, however, confined itself to naming bankruptcy as being among the other grounds for the liquidation of an enterprise, providing that in instances of bankruptcy the liquidation is to be effectuated by decision of a court.

---

[159]   See Articles 32 and 33, USSR Law on Banks and Bank Activities, adopted 11 December 1990. *Vedomosti SND SSSR* (1990), no. 52, item 1155.

[160]   Article 24. *Vedomosti SND RSFSR* (1990), no. 30, item 418.

[161]   Article 37. Adopted 4 June 1990. *Vedomosti SND SSSR* (1990), no. 25, item 460. Transl. in W. E. Butler (ed.), *Basic Documents on the Soviet Legal System* (2d ed., 1991), p. 317.

5. In civil legislation the concept "insuperable force" is extensively used, chiefly with respect to individual types of contracts and delictual obligations. There exists a legal definition of insuperable force. Although it is incorporated in the union republic civil codes on periods of limitation, it also is used when deciding the question of responsibility. Article 85 of the RSFSR Civil Code and analogous articles of the other union republic civil codes define insuperable force as an "extraordinary and unavoidable event under particular conditions." It follows from this that a phenomenon of an elemental character, just as any other event, may be deemed to be insuperable force only on condition that it satisfies both indiciae contained in Article 85: (1) extraordinary; and (2) unavoidable. Events must be assessed in the light of specific situations; a buran storm in Central Asia is insuperable force, but not in Siberia.

6. A special 1990 USSR Law on the Legal Regime of an Extraordinary Situation has been adopted which determines the reasons for which an extraordinary situation may be declared (to ensure the safety of citizens in natural calamities, large wrecks or accidents, epidemics, epizootics, mass disorders) and who has the right to introduce it (on the territory of the USSR as a whole, the USSR Supreme Soviet; in individual localities, the republic supreme soviet, and at the request of the last or with its consent, the President of the USSR).[162] Among the measures which may be introduced are the making of changes in the plans of enterprises and organisations, the establishment of a special work regime for them; and

---

[162]   Adopted 30 April 1990. *Vedomosti SND SSSR* (1990), no. 16, item 250; transl. in W. E. Butler (ed.), *Basic Documents on the Soviet Legal System* (2d ed., 1991), pp. 51-55. The RSFSR adopted an analogous law in 1991.

deciding other questions of economic activity. All these are matters directly connected with investment activity.

7. Article 3(2) of the FPInvA (see Commentary thereto) prohibits investing in specified objects. The last paragraph of point 3 of this Article is directly linked to Article 3(2) because it contains the sanctions applicable if the prohibition is violated. Here we encounter an artifically split norm: the disposition is placed in Article 3(2), and the sanction in Article 20. Accordingly, the list of grounds for the application of the sanction is fully consistent with that set out in Article 3.

The sanction referred to may be applied only to an investor because only he is a potential violator of the prohibition. The essence of the sanction is that the customer or investor who has violated the prohibition not only will not achieve his purpose (construction can not continue) but will also be obliged to compensate the participant for the value of the work performed irrespective whether he uses the result of the work.

There are two alternative consequences: either termination or suspension of construction. The choice belongs to the competent State agency which applies the sanction. However, this choice is predetermined by objective circumstances. If an investor has the possiblity to eliminate the obstacles specified in Article 3 (violation of existing sanitary-hygienic and ecological rules, or the enterprise is built without the necessary purification installations, and others) it is advisable to suspend construction. If it turns out that the defects discovered can not be eliminated (they are dangerous to human life or health), the sanction must obviously be termination of construction.

There do not presently exist special rules applicable to the situations referred to in the FPInvA. For this reason one should be guided by the general norms devoted to the consequences of the suspension or termination of construction.

Article 21: Responsibility of Subjects of Investment Activity

In the event of the failure to comply with contractual obligations, the subjects of investment activity shall bear property and other responsibility provided for by legislation and the contracts concluded.

The payment of fines and penalties for a violation of the conditions of contracts, as well as compensation for losses caused, shall not relieve the guilty party from fulfilling obligations unless provided otherwise by law or contract.

1. The 1961 FPCivL contains general norms concerning responsibility for a violation of obligations, including contractual, as well as special norms devoted to responsibility for a violation of obligations arising from individual types of contracts.

General norms on civil law responsibility may roughly be characterised as follows:

- one of the grounds for responsibility to ensue for the failure to perform or for the improper performance of obligations is, unless provided otherwise by law or contract, the fault of the debtor. The special case of responsibility without fault is delay: the debtor who has allowed the delay of performance must be liable also for that which has accidentally ensued during the delay in performing the obligation;

-    the debtor is liable for the actions of third persons to whom the performance of an obligation has been entrusted. This means in regard to the situation considered here that a general independent-work contractor must bear responsibility to a customer for actions of a sub-independent-work contractor (the latter fulfils work at the instruction of the general independent-work contractor), and is responsible to the subindependent-work contractor for the actions of the customer (for example, untimely payment for work performed).

And although the respective norm of the 1961 FPCivL (Article 38) allows the possibility of establishing direct responsibility in a law for a third person to a creditor, legislative acts in the domain of capital construction, including the present Law, do not make provision for such an exception. Consequently, the customer and subindependent-work contractor may not present any demands to one another;

-    if both parties are guilty of violating an obligation (the fault of the creditor may, in particular, be expressed in the fact that his actions have increased the losses which arose as a consequence of the violation of the obligation by the debtor), the principle of mixed responsibility applies. It is expressed in the fact that a jurisdictional organ (court, arbitrazh court, arbitration court) has the right respectively to reduce the extent of responsibility of the debtor;

-    a violation of an obligation entails the necessity to compensate losses (see the Commentary to Article 20 on the composition of losses);

-    if responsibility is provided for in the form of a penalty (or fine), according to the general rule in such instances the losses are compensated only in that part which has not been covered by the penalty (the so-called "set-off" penalty). One of three types of penalty may be established in a law or contract: fine [*shtraf*] (losses are recovered in full without setting off the amount of penalty received); exclusive (payment of the penalty relieves from the need to compensate any losses whatsoever); or alternative (a creditor has the right to demand either the payment of the penalty or compensation of losses. Having chosen one of these sanctions, the creditor loses his right to the other);

-    the possibility of establishing by USSR or republic legislation limited responsibility for individual types of obligations is permitted.[163] Joint enterprises with the participation of foreign capital would thus be at liberty to conclude contracts containing provisions limiting responsibility, and the same would be true of a foreign firm effectuating investment activity in the USSR and concluding contracts in that connection.

2.   The   Rules   concerning   Independent-Work Contracts for Capital Construction contain an extensive list of   fine   sanctions   applicable   to   a   customer   or independent-work   contractor   who   did   not   perform properly.   Before   perestroika   all   such   sanctions automatically extended to contracting parties irrespective of whether those norms were set out in the contract or not. Any provision of such a contract contrary to those norms was considered to be void.

The situation has substantially changed. The norms of such rules concerning sanctions are regarded as imperative,

---

[163]   Article 70, 1991 FPCivL, in W. E. Butler (intro. & transl.), *The USSR Fundamental Principles of Civil Legislation* (1991); Article 36, 1961 FPCivL, in W. E. Butler (comp. & transl.), *The Soviet Legal System: Legislation and Documentation* (1978), pp. 404-405.

that is, as absolutely binding upon the parties, only when the construction is effectuated at the expense of capital investments from the centralised funds of the ministry or department or from the budget or on the basis of a State order. When the contract is concluded at the discretion of the parties, irrespective of whether the parties are socialist organisations or are joint enterprises or foreign firms effectuating investments in the USSR, the provisions concerning sanctions are not imperative or even dispositive. The parties themselves determine the consequences of a breach of the contract. Consequently, the section of the Rules regarding property responsibility is operational only when the contract expressly refers to the Rules.

Under perestroika the situations when the parties are obliged to conclude a contract are fewer in number, and in those instances the Rules provide for responsibility for a violation of so-called contractual obligations. They have in view responsibility for evading the conclusion of a contract (a penalty of 0.05% per day, but not exceeding 1,000 rubles), as well as the untimely transfer of design-estimate documentation (a fine of 250 rubles per day).

Moreover, each contracting party bears property responsibility for a violation of specified circumstances according to the contract. The customer is liable for a delay in the delivery of materials and equipment which by virtue of the contract he must deliver to an independent-work contractor (8% of the value of the materials and equipment not transferred within the period), for the delivery of incomplete equipment (20% of the value of the incomplete set), for delay in accepting work completed (0.05% per day of the value of all construction-assembly work, but not less than 150 nor more than 500 rubles per day), and for delay in paying for work completed (the same rate and limits as for delay in accepting work completed).

In turn, the independent-work contractor is liable for the untimely failure to fulfil construction or assembly work through his fault (penalty of 0.05% of their estimate value per day, but not exceeding 100 rubles per day) or for delay in rectifying defects discovered within the guarantee periods (100 rubles for each day of delay).[164] The low domestic value of the purchasing power of the ruble sometimes results in penalties being deliberately incurred while resources are diverted more profitably; it is less expensive to pay the penalty. If defects discovered during the guarantee period are not eliminated by the independent-work contractor, the customer may do so himself, in which case the latter may be compensated for the cost of the work and receive a fine equivalent to 50% of the amount.

3. The Rules on Contracts for the Fulfilment of Design and Survey Work provide equal responsibility for the independent-work contractor (for the untimely fulfilment of work) and the customer (for the untimely issuance of basic design data to the independent-work contractor): a penalty of 0.01% per day, but after thirty days have elapsed the recovery of the penalty is terminated and further responsibility is limited to payment of a penalty equal to 1% of the value of the respective work.

The 1959 Rules were augmented in 1967 by yet another sanction: a design organisation is obliged to eliminate the design defects discovered at its own expense within the shortest technically possible period agreed with

[164] The existing guarantee periods are rather brief: one year for general construction work; six months for assembled equipment; one heating season for central heating, and the like. The longest period is two years, for the construction of dwelling houses.

the customer. If this is not done, a penalty is due in the amount of 4% of the value of work which should have been fulfilled. Payment of the penalty is not a substitute for specific performance. Another innovation introduced in 1967 was to impose on the independent-work contractor the duty to pay compensation for losses caused. But this duty of compensation was limited: the design organisation must compensate losses in full, but not exceeding the value of the work provided for by the contract relating to drawing up the construction design, and even then not the entire design but only that portion which appertains to the specific shop, building, or installation in which the defects were discovered. Thus the risk of poor quality design passes in significant measure to the customer.

4. The Statute on Contracts for the Creation (or Transfer) of a Scientific-Technical Product confines itself, with regard to responsibility, to a reference to prevailing legislation. This means that in the absence of any other indications in the contract a breach thereof must entail compensation to the contracting party for losses without any limitations. As a result it turns out that the performer of scientific research work bears greater responsibility than a designer, although the former's work is more creative and may involve greater risk. Passing the risk in these relations from the customer to the independent-work contractor is not always advantageous to the customer since the independent-work contractor will be inclined to perform the work in a routine manner with lower risk. When there is little competition amongst those who perform such work, this negative circumstance should not be overlooked. In future one might expect as regards this contract a narrowing of the responsibility of he who performs the work so that the possible risk would be distributed more equally among the parties.

5. Paragraph two of this Article consolidates the principle of specific performance of obligations, reproducing the general rule set out in the 1961 FPCivL,[165] but not included in the 1991 FPCivL. The principle is limited in application by the corresponding principle of "impossibility of performance." If the impossibility of performance has arisen -- physical, legal, and even economic under certain circumstances -- through the fault of one of the parties, that party is liable to the contracting party. When performance is impossible by reason of circumstances for which the debtor is not liable, the obligation terminates.[166] Some believe, however, that there are grounds for reviewing this rule so that the obligation would terminate only when none of the parties could be brought to responsibility.

---

[165]   Article 36. Transl. in W. E. Butler (comp. & transl.), *The Soviet Legal System: Legislation and Documentation* (1978), pp. 404-405.

[166]   Article 235, 1964 RSFSR Civil Code, and analogous articles in the other union republic civil codes. The same rule is reproduced in Article 73(3) of the 1991 FPCivL. See W. E. Butler (intro. & transl.), *The USSR Fundamental Principles of Civil Legislation* (1991).

Article 22: Responsibility When Realising State Order

1. In the event of the failure to perform or the improper performance of obligations accepted with regard to the fulfilment of an order of the State or of the duties imposed on legal grounds, State agencies of all levels shall bear property responsibility for their obligations to subjects of investment activities. In the event the assets of these agencies are insufficient, damage shall be compensated respectively by the USSR, the union or autonomous republic, or local soviet of people's deputies whose agency did not perform or who improperly performed their obligations. The guilty officials shall bear personal responsibility in accordance with prevailing legislation.

2. Union and republic State agencies shall bear mutual property responsibility for the failure to perform or the improper performance of obligations connected with the realisation of Union orders of the State, compensating the damage caused, including lost advantage.

3. Participants of investment activity shall bear property responsibility to the investor State for the realisation of orders of the State in the procedure established by legislation and contracts concluded.

1.   Point 1 of this Article, and indeed the Article as a whole, are devoted to the responsibility of agencies which have issued an order to its addressees, as well as of the higher and inferior agencies of State power and administration for a violation of their mutual duties connected with bringing the State order to those who perform it.

2.   The 1987 USSR Law on the State Enterprise (repealed on 7 March 1991) provided that a State order sent by a superior agency to an enterprise must be directly incorporated by the latter in its Plan. In issuing a State order, the ministry or department is effectuating its administrative competence relative to the enterprise which is the addressee of the order. This meant that relations which are formed between those two persons -- the agency which issued the State order and the addressee -- are based on the principles of power and subordination. These legal relations are administrative and, consequently, by virtue of Article 2 of the FPCivL are outside the framework of civil law.[167] However, the civil law institute of delictual responsibility is of a universal character in the sense that in using the sanction of compensation for losses one is capable of ensuring the performance of duties regulated by any other branch of law and not only civil law, on condition that the infringement has been expressed in the causing of property harm and an absolute right is the object thereof.[168]

---

[167]   Article 2, paragraph three, of the 1961 FPCivL provides: "USSR and union republic civil legislation shall not apply to property relations based on the administrative subordination of one party to another, nor to tax and budget relations." Article 2 of the 1964 RSFSR Civil Code contains an identical formulation in substance. Article 1(4) of the 1991 FPCivL broadens the formula slightly, but adds the qualification "... except for instances provided for by USSR and republic legislation." See W. E. Butler (intro. & transl.), *The USSR Fundamental Principles of Civil Legislation* (1991).

It is precisely this situation which is formed when a State order is issued. Thus, there is every basis to regard the issuance of an order as a special instance of those various situations which fall under the operation of Article 89 of the 1961 FPCivL (Responsibility for Harm Caused by the Illegal Activities of State and Social Organisations, as well as Officials) and Article 127, 1991 FPCivL.[169] On the application of this Article in combination with Article 88, paras. one and two, of the 1961 FPCivL and Article 126, 1991 FPCivL, see the Commentary to Article 20; the same view substantiates the subsidiary responsibility of the Union, a republic, or local agencies of power for the actions of agencies which have caused harm to a victim.

The content of these obligations was strengthened in the Provisional Statute on the Procedure for Issuing State Orders for 1989 and 1990, confirmed by Decree of the USSR Council of Ministers of 25 July 1988.[170] It provided that State orders are issued to customers and independent-work contractors for the introduction into operation of major production capacities at the expense of

---

[168]   See V. T. Smirnov and A. A. Sobchak, *Obshchee uchenie o deliktnykh obiazatel'stvakh* (1983), p. 27.

[169]   Article 89, paragraph one, of the FPCivL provides, as amended: "Harm caused to a citizen by the illegal actions of State and social organisations, and also by officials when they are executing their employment duties in the domain of administrative management, shall be compensated on the general bases (Article 88 of the present Fundamental Principles) unless otherwise provided by law.

For harm caused by such actions to organisations, responsibility shall ensue in the procedure established by law."

Svod zakonov SSSR, II, 31; transl. in W. E. Butler, *Collected Legislation of the USSR and Constituent Union Republics* (1979-). The language quoted corresponds to Article 446, as amended 24 February 1987, of the RSFSR Civil Code. See *Grazhdanskii kodeks RSFSR (s postateinymi materialami)* (1990), p. 133. For Articles 126 and 127, 1991 FPCivL, see W. E. Butler (intro. & transl.), *The USSR Fundamental Principles of Civil Legislation* (1991).

[170]   *SP SSSR* (1988), no. 26, item 71.

State centralised capital investments. They also may be issued in instances when construction must be effectuated at the expense of assets of enterprises, on condition that the latter themselves raise the question that it is essential to issue the order. The agency from which the State order directly emanates (ministry, department, inter-branch State association) assumes the obligation to provide the enterprise with ceiling quotas for major material-technical resources and ceiling quotas for construction and assembly work (in both instances the ceiling quota means the right on the part of to whomever it is issued to demand from the supplier enterprise or respective independent-work contractor the conclusion of a respective contract), and also to decide questions connected with the conclusion of contracts in execution of the order. If one of the addressees of the State order refuses to conclude the contract, the agency which issued the order must make necessary changes therein or annul it. If it turns out that the change of or annulment of the State order has caused the enterprise material loss, it must be compensated at the expense of centralised funds and reserves of the ministry or department.

The Provisional Statute lapsed in accordance with its terms and so far has not been replaced by another. However, this is no obstacle to a victim bringing suits in the situations specified therein concerning compensation for harm, relying on Article 89 of the 1961 FPCivL, or from 1 January 1992, Article 127 of the 1991 FPCivL.

3. The wording of Article 89 of the 1961 FPCivL and 1991 FPCivL may justify a distinction between harm caused through the fault of agencies, first, and through the fault of their officials, second. In fact, however, the wording of the norm is unsatisfactory since in all instances

the responsibility for the harm caused in the sphere of administrative management is borne by the agency acting in the capacity of a juridical person. From the standpoint of civil law, the official of a ministry or department and other administrative agencies is in no way distinct from the workers thereof. That is why in the case of harm caused by officials one should be guided, in addition to Article 89 of the 1961 FPCivL, also by paragraph three of the Article 88, 1961 FPCivL (Article 126[3], 1991 FPCivL), which provides that an organisation (in this case, an agency) is obliged to compensate for harm caused through the fault of its workers when they perform their labour or employment duties.[171] The fault of any worker is deemed to be the fault of the juridical person (or agency, organisation).

The peculiarities of the functions effectuated by the person directly causing the harm is of no significance. The responsibility of a juridical person may be the result of the improper performance by a worker of his actual actions (driver of an automobile belonging to the ministry during work hours collides with a pedestrian) or of his legal actions (official signs a State order directed to an enterprise and thereby imparts legal force to the respective document). Article 88, paragraph three, of the 1961 FPCivL (Article 126[2], 1991 FPCivL) enables, a contrario, the conclusion to be drawn that the official of a superior agency may bear direct responsibility to the enterprise only for his personal actions, that is, those which are not connected with the performance of employment duties.

---

[171]   As amended 23 May 1986, Article 88, paragraph three, of the FPCivL provides that: "An organisation shall be obliged to compensate caused through the fault of its workers when they are performing their labour (or employment) duties." *Svod zakonov SSSR*, II, 31. This provision is reproduced verbatim as Article 445 of the RSFSR Civil Code. See *Grazhdanskii kodeks RSFSR (s postateinymi materialami)* (1990), p. 132. For Article 126(2), 1991 FPCivL, see W. E. Butler (intro. & transl.), *The USSR Fundamental Principles of Civil Legislation* (1991).

4. The personal responsibility of a guilty official referred to in this Point of the Article can take one of three forms, each of which is outside the civil law: that is, (1) material; (2) disciplinary; and (3) criminal. An official bears material responsibility to the agency with which he is connected by labour relations. This responsibility is of a regressive character; it ensues only after the agency pays the respective amount to the victim and is expressed in a demand addressed to the official to compensate the amount paid by reason of his fault. This is a regressive obligation in which the agency which issued the State order is the regressant and the official is the regressee subordinated to the operation of labour law, which means a significant limitation of responsibility. By virtue of Article 49 of the FPLabL the limitations are expressed in the fact that, first, material responsibility is allowed only "within the amount of direct contractual damage" (thus excluding the need to compensate for lost advantage) and, second, the general rule that it may not exceed the monthly earnings of the person (full material responsibility occurs only in instances expressly specified in law, chiefly in connection with the performance of activities containing the indicia of a crime).

The disciplinary responsibility of an official includes various types of sanction, from a reprimand up to dismissal. It is applied by decision of the director of the organisation or agency with which the worker is in labour relations or by the superior organisation. If certain prerequisites are present, an official also may bear criminal responsibility. This has in view the commission of so-called official crimes. These are chiefly: official forgery (the entry by an official for mercenary purposes or other personal motives of knowingly false information in official documents, the falsification, erasure, or misdating, and likewise the drawing up and issuance by him of knowingly false documents, or the entry of knowingly false entries in a book), as set out in Article 175, RSFSR Criminal Code; neglect (the nonfulfilment or the improper fulfilment by an official of his duties as a consequence of a careless or unconscientious attitude toward them), as set out in Article 172, RSFSR Criminal Code; and the exceeding of power or of official powers (the intentional commission by an official of actions which clearly exceed the limits of the rights and powers granted to the official by law),[172] as set out in Article 171, RSFSR Criminal Code.[173]

5. Point 2 of this Article provides for a special type of sanctions which are connected with certain relations arising between State agencies of the USSR and the republics in theprocess of notifying a Union order to the executor of that order. The Point contemplates that satisfaction of a demand concerning compensation of losses declared by an inferior agency against a superior agency is permitted. The most typical situation would be regressive demands caused by the fact that through the fault of a Union agency a republic agency must compensate losses to an enterprise. In turn, a Union agency has the right to bring demands against a republic agency if a State order is not realised through the fault of the latter.

---

[172]   Criminal responsibility for neglect and for exceeding rights and powers ensues only when the respective actions have caused material harm to State or social interests.

[173]   The RSFSR Criminal Code was confirmed by a Law of the RSFSR Supreme Soviet on 27 October 1960 and been amended numerous times. The most recent English translation is in W. E. Butler (ed.), *Basic Documents on the Soviet Legal System* (1983), pp. 295-394, as amended to 1 August 1983. Chapter VII of the Code, Articles 170 to 175-1, is devoted to "Official Crimes." The Criminal Code is to be replaced in the near future.

6. Point 3 of this Article suggests that it is principally concerned with a special situation when the participant of an investment concludes an independent-work contract for capital construction or other contract directly with the State as such, that is, with the USSR or a republic. It should be borne in mind, however, that although the USSR and a republic are subjects of civil law in equal measure and respectively may participate in civil turnover, they realise their legal capacity rarely and in any case ordinarily in links not connected with the conclusion of investment contracts.[174] Usually the respective amounts of investments are allocated to State agencies, organisations, and enterprises, which conclude contracts with the participants of investment activity and bear responsibility to one another arising from the contract binding them. So far the legislator has not provided any special procedure for presenting respective demands when investments are effectuated by the State as such.

7. Directly relevant to Point 3 of this Article is the practice of recent years whereby in the event of a violation of contractual obligations both contracting parties, that is, the customer organisation and independent-work contractor, must contribute a specified amount to the budget. The amount of and the grounds for such penalties are defined by the Government of the USSR. Thus, Decree No. 809 of the USSR Council of Ministers of 30 September 1989, "On Certain Measures Regarding Improvement of the Status of Affairs in Capital Construction," provided that in the event of the failure to comply with the periods specified in independent-work contracts for the introduction into operation of objects

---

[174] M. I. Braginskii, *The Soviet State as a Subject of Civil Law* (1988), pp. 164-188.

which are erected at the expense of State capital investments and centralised funds of ministries and departments, payments to the budget must be made at the rate of 0.5% for each month of violation of the periods for the introduction of the object into operation until it was actually in operation (the penalty is calculated for the customer against the value of the basic funds and for the independent-work contractor, against the value of the construction and assembly work regarding the objects not introduced into operation).[175] Analogous sanctions are levied for the budget also with regard to construction sites effectuated at the expense of assets of an enterprise, though at a significantly lower rate (6% annually of the value of the objects not introduced into operation).

These sanctions emerged in legislation in connection with the fact that the customer and independent-work contractor do not always have enough interest in finishing construction work on time. In our view these measures are very doubtful. It is evident that with the normal development of market relations their participants will conclude contracts between themselves only on condition that they are interested in receiving the results of the work (customer) and being paid (independent-work contractor). For this reason in a genuine market there is no need to artificially stimulate the contracting parties. The fact that it became necessary to coerce the contractor to complete construction is an aberration of commodity relations. If it does become essential to intensify the responsibility of the contractor, a more effective means can be chosen: increase the level of contractual sanctions. Pumping money into the budget in this form is nothing other than reviving means of pressure inherent in the administrative-command system.

---

[175]   *SP SSSR* (1989), no. 33, item 149.

No doubt the Government of the RSFSR was influenced in this respect when it provided that the USSR Decree of 30 September 1989 was not operative on the territory of the Russian Federation.

Article 23: Protection of Investments

1. The State shall guarantee the protection of investments irrespective of the forms of ownership, as well as foreign investments. The protection of investments shall be ensured by legislation of the USSR, the union and autonomous republics, and agreements between them. In so doing, an equal regime of investors shall be ensured, including foreign investors, which precludes the application of measures of a discriminatory character that could obstruct the administration of investments, their use and liquidation, as well as provide for the conditions and procedure for the export of invested valuables and results of investments.

2. Investments may not be, without compensation, nationalised, requisitioned nor measures taken with regard to them equivalent in consequences. Such measures may be applied only on the basis of legislative acts of the USSR and union and autonomous republics, with compensation to the investor in full for losses caused in connection with the termination of investment activity. The procedure for compensation of losses to an investor shall be determined in the said acts.

Special purpose bank deposits, stocks, and other securities contributed or acquired by investors, payments for acquired property or for lease rights shall, in instances of their seizure in accordance with legislative acts of the USSR and union and autonomous republics, be compensated to investors, except for amounts which prove to be used or lost as a result of the actions of the investors themselves or undertaken with their participation.

3. Disputes arising as a result of the effectuation of investment activity shall be considered respectively by a court, State Arbitrazh, or arbitration court.

4. Disputes concerning the failure to fulfil or the improper performance of obligations arising from contracts affecting investment activity between union and republic agencies of administration, agencies of administration of union and autonomous republics, as well as between republics, shall be considered by way of arbitral examination or by State Arbitrazh of the USSR.

5. Investments may, and in the instances provided for by law must, be insured.

1. Investments are the investing of specified property in various forms. They are either things (equipment, building, installations, securities, and the like) or rights arising from a contract for the lease of land or a building, rights to intellectual valuables, and the like (see Commentary to Article 1). Of great importance for investment protection in whatever form the investments take are the means considered above, including demands for compensation of losses in connection with the creation of a new law (see Commentary to Article 20) or the

issuance of an unlawful act in the sphere of administrative management (see Commentary to Articles 20, 21, and 22), as well as deeming the act of an agency of administration to be void (see Commentary to Article 20).

The above enumerated means of protecting the rights of an investor are basically mandatory. However, the fact that "things" comprise all or part of an investment presupposes the possibility of using as well the traditional means of protecting the rights of an owner, such as *nugatory* suits to eliminate any violations of the rights of an owner even though such violations were not linked with a deprivation of possession, and vindication suits to demand and obtain an owner's property from the illegal possession of another. Satisfying a vindication suit depends upon whether the person to whom it is addressed was an acquirer *in good faith* or *not in good faith* (the latter is whether he knew or at least should have known that he from whom he acquired the thing did not have the right to alienate it, whereas in good faith he did not know this and should not have known it). A thing may be demanded and obtained from an acquirer not in good faith in all instances, but from an acquirer in good faith only under the circumstances specified in the 1961 FPCivL (Article 28): an owner lost the thing in dispute or it was stolen from him, or the thing was lost by a person to whom the owner voluntarily entrusted the thing (goods warehouse, left luggage room for passengers, and the like). The lawful possessor of a thing (lessee, pledgeholder, and others) has the right to bring nugatory and vindication suits on the same conditions, in addition to an owner. The same principle has been retained in Article 54, 1991 FPCivL.

2. This point consolidates the principle of equal protection of investments irrespective of the type of

ownership, and accordingly discrimination in any possible form is prohibited. The question arises in this connection of the fate of privileges established by the 1961 FPCivL (Article 28) intended to protect a specific category of owners. State, cooperative, and social organisations, as an exception to the aforesaid rules, were granted the possibility of unlimited vindication. This meant it was necessary to satisfy demands concerning the return of a thing irrespective of whether the acquirer was in good faith or not. Moreover, the demands of State organisations for the return of a thing were not impaired by the periods of limitation (an exception is vindication suits by one State organisation against another such State organisation). The 1991 FPCivL excluded this preferential regime for State, cooperative, and social organisations.

3. Legislation in force contains special norms concerning the protection of foreign investments, chiefly with respect to joint enterprises with the participation of foreign capital. Relevant here are individual points of the Decree of the USSR Council of Ministers of 13 January 1987, No. 49, on the procedure for creating joint enterprises with the participation of Soviet organisations and firms of capitalist and developing countries.[176] That Decree provides that the property of joint enterprises is not subject to requisition or confiscation in an administrative proceeding and established the national regime for the protection of property rights of a joint enterprise (to them extends a special preferential regime of protection which does not yet exist for State organisations); a foreign participant of a joint enterprise is guaranteed the remittance abroad in foreign hard currency the amounts

---

[176]   *SP SSSR* (1987), no. 9, item 40; transl. as amended in W. E. Butler (ed.), *Basic Documents on the Soviet Legal System* (2d ed., 1991), pp. 475-484.

due him as a result of the distribution of profit. When the enterprise is liquidated or a foreign participant withdraws therefrom, the foreign participant receives the right to a return of his contribution in monetary or goods form with regard to the residual value (however, only after paying obligations to Soviet participants of the joint enterprise and third persons).

All the same, it should be recognised that the existing guarantees for joint enterprises and their foreign participants may prove to be inadequate, especially in instances when a foreign investor is a party against the State as such, which enjoys immunity, including judicial immunity. Further, by Edict of the President of the USSR "On Foreign Investments" (translated as an Annex to this Commentary) the possibility is provided for the creation of enterprises in which 100% of the capital belongs to a foreign investor. It is necessary in this connection to guarantee the interests of all foreign investors effectuating economic activity in the USSR.

Some such guarantees are contained in the Edict itself: granting the national regime to foreign investors in the USSR, freedom to reinvest, the possibility of using Soviet currency, as well as the transfer of hard currency profit abroad (the latter with the material reservation: "in the procedure established by law"). The Edict was strengthened and elaborated by investment guarantee provisions in the 1991 FPForInv (see Annexe 3). The practice of individual republics, who in this sense anticipated the USSR, is worthy of attention. The Law "On Foreign Investments in the Kazakh SSR" provided that the profit received in the republic may be freely reinvested on its territory, that the protection and effectuation of the rights of intellectual property shall be ensured in the Kazakh SSR in accordance with republic legislation, that the republic guarantees foreign investors the right to freely transfer abroad revenues from their activities and the liquidation of a juridical person with foreign participation, and also from the sale of its share in the said enterprises.

4. National legislation has been reinforced and in some cases extended by international agreements of the USSR on the protection of capital investments. By 29 May 1991 fourteen such agreements had been ratified by the USSR.[177]

While each agreement has distinctive features, they all coincide in their points of departure. They consolidate the duty of States-parties to refrain from expropriation, nationalisation, and other analogous measures; such measures might be effectuated only in exceptional instances while complying with three conditions: first, the actions of the State must not be of a discriminatory character; second, they must be provided for by legislation of the State which effectuated those actions; and third, it is mandatory to pay full compensation to the investor. By compensation is understood reimbursement of the real value of the capital investments, taking into account world prices, and in freely convertible currency. Of special significance is the inclusion in the agreements of norms which allow for the possibility of the settlement of disputes in a commercial court which arise between the foreign investor and the State-party on whose territory the capital investment was effectuated. The USSR has thereby waived its immunity within these strictly defined limits. The same, of course, also applies to the other State-party to the Agreement.

---

[177]   Among the signatories are Belgium with Luxembourg, Finland, United Kingdom, Germany, France, Italy, Canada, Netherlands, Austria, China, South Korea, and Spain.

5. Point 2 of this Article names "nationalisation" and "requisition" amongst the measures which a State may not effectuate. The expression "measures taken with regard to them equal in consequences" would clearly include confiscation and sequestration.

6. The concepts of "requisition" and "confiscation" are defined in a special Article of the union republic civil codes (especially Article 149, RSFSR Civil Code). Requisition is deemed to be the "seizure by the State of property from a owner for State or social interests with payment of compensation," and confiscation is the "seizure by the State without compensation of property as a sanction for a violation of law." A comparison of the definitions in the Civil Code with the present Article shows that the version of the last is not entirely satisfactory. As is evident from the definition, requisition always presupposes compensation. This means that the reference to the fact that requisition must invariably be done with compensation has no meaning (seizure without payment in general is not requisition).

7. In the event of confiscation or requisition, the assessment is effectuated by a commission composed of representatives of financial agencies and organisations which will receive or realise this property. Appeals against the unlawfulness of the confiscation and requisition must be directed to the agency superior to the agency which issued the respective decree. If the appeal is deemed to be well-founded, the property is returned in kind, but if it already has been realised, the respective amount due is to be paid from the union, republic, or local budget, depending upon to whom the value of the confiscated

property was credited. Citizens and juridical persons who have suffered from an unfounded confiscation or requisition have the right to bring suit for compensation of losses against the agency whose official rendered the decree. Satisfaction of the respective demand is effectuated within the framework of Article 89 of the FPCivL or Article 127, 1991 FPCivL (see Commentary to Articles 20 and 22).

8.   In the early years of Soviet power property was intensively nationalised, including land, factories and plants, buildings, and others. Later nationalisation lost its importance as one of the principal sources of creating State ownership. The last mention of it is to be found in the Statute on the Procedure for Registering and Using Nationalised, Confiscated, Escheated, and Masterless Property.[178] Worthy of attention is the fact that the Instruction of the USSR Ministry of Finances of 30 June 1956 concerning the procedure for applying the Statute did not mention norms on nationalisation. The resuscitation of this notion in legislation now is due exclusively to the admission of foreign capital.

Nationalisation is combined with confiscation and requisition because it represents the initial means for the right of ownership to arise.[179] For this reason it is acknowledged that only rights pass to the State in such instances, and not the duties of the former owners. Continuing the comparison, it should be noted that nationalisation is similar in some respects to confiscation (without compensation) and in others to requisition (not connected with unlawful behaviour of the owner). And

[178]   Confirmed by the Government of the USSR on 13 April 1943. *SP SSSR* (1943), no. 6, item 98.

[179]   See D. M. Genkin, *Pravo sobstvennosti v SSSR* (1961), p. 128ff.

there is another characteristic which draws nationalisation closer to requisition: unlike confiscation, which always is based on an individual act (decree of a court or other competent agency with respect to the particular property), requisition and nationalisation usually are provided for by a general act. Thus, in the early years after the Revolution the nationalisation of all enterprises of a specified branch was effectuated, all enterprises whose numbers of workers exceeded an established maximum, and the like. During the Second World War a Decree of the Government of the USSR was published on the requisition of all radios from Soviet citizens.

9.   Point 2 of this Article, clearly having requisition in mind, provides for full compensation of losses (the position of Kazakh SSR legislation with respect to foreign investments is the same). It thus goes farther than the Civil Code, which as already noted limits itself to a demand for payment of the value of the requisitioned property.

Since in the present FPInvA there are no limitations with regard to the losses subject to compensation, it should be recognised that compensation, in full conformity with the general norms of the FPCivL (Article 36), includes both positive loss and lost advantage (revenues not received).

10. Although not mentioned in USSR legislation, certain republic legislative acts refer to sequestration of property. They have in view not so much sequestration during hostilities, but the distraint of property of an investor who wishes to withdraw his investment pending the settlement of any civil obligations within the Soviet Union. RSFSR legislation on the economic zones in

Nakhodka and Sakhalin makes specific reference to sequestration.

11. Paragraph two of point 2 reflects the specific features of compensation with regard to securities and certain other types of property. The basic points of departure in this event correspond to those consolidated in paragraph one of this same point.

12. In accordance with prevailing norms:

- disputes between socialist organisations, except for collective farms, must be decided by State Arbitrazh, which pursuant to amendments to the USSR Constitution in December 1990 was transformed into the Supreme Arbitrazh Court of the USSR;[180]

- disputes between joint enterprises with the participation of foreign capital and Soviet organisations, joint enterprises situated on the territory of the USSR between themselves, and disputes between participants of a joint enterprise with regard to questions connected with its activity (and evidently also disputes between participants and the joint enterprise) are all considered in courts of the USSR or, by arrangement of the parties, in an arbitration tribunal. Courts for these purposes includes the Supreme Arbitrazh Court and inferior courts;

- a permanent arbitration court functions in the Soviet Union: the Arbitration Court attached to the Chamber of Commerce and Industry of the USSR. The Statute on that agency provides that it considers disputes which arise from contracts and other civil-law relations

---

[180] The Law on the USSR Supreme Arbitrazh Court was adopted 17 May 1991. See *Izvestiia*, 4 June 1991, p. 2, cols. 1-6.

when foreign trade and other international and scientific-technical links are effectuated;[181]

- on the territory of the Kazakh SSR the rule is that disputes with the participation of enterprises in which foreign capital participates wholly or in part shall be settled either by courts, or by State Arbitrazh, or by arbitration tribunals.

13. As regards Point 4 of this Law, all disputes relating to economic questions, including compensation of losses, between the USSR and the union and autonomous republics, autonomous regions and national areas, are considered by way of arbitration or by the USSR Supreme Court.[182]

14. As regards Point 5 of this Law, compulsory insurance extends to a rather extensive range of property of collective farms, State farms, and other agricultural enterprises, as well as dwelling houses, and large domestic livestock belonging to citizens. Pursuant to Article 14 of Decree No. 49 of 13 January 1987 on the creation of joint enterprises,[183] a joint enterprise is obliged to insure its property in insurance agencies of the USSR; however, the insurance of risks may be done voluntarily by joint enterprises. In the Kazakh SSR both the risks and the

---

[181]   For the Statute of this Court, see *Vedomosti SSSR* (1987), no. 50, item 806; transl. in W. E. Butler, *Arbitration in the Soviet Union* (1989), pp. 25-26.

[182]   See the Law on Basic Principles of Economic Relations of the USSR and Union and Autonomous Republics, adopted 10 April 1990. *Vedomosti SND SSSR* (1990), no. 16, item 270; transl. in W. E. Butler (ed.), *Basic Documents on the Soviet Legal System* (2d ed., 1991), pp. 235-242.

[183]   Translated in W. E. Butler (ed.), *Basic Documents on the Soviet Legal System* (2d ed., 1991), pp. 475-484

property of joint enterprises with foreign participation is insured at their discretion. The 1991 FPForInv allows foreign investors to insure property and risks by arrangement and at their discretion.

The State monopoly of insurance is being disbanded in the Soviet Union. Insurance companies structured on corporate principles, with and without the participation of State capital, have emerged[184].

---

[184]   See the Decree of the USSR Cabinet of Ministers, no. 397, of 23 June 1991, "On Measures of State Regulation of Insurance Activity" and the Decree no. 421 of 30 June 1991 "On the Creation of the All-Union State Insurance Commercial Organisation." The prohibition against joint enterprises entering the insurance business in the USSR was repealed. *SP SSSR* (1991), no. 18-19, items 75 and 76.

ANNEXES

Annexes

ON THE INTRODUCTION INTO EFFECT OF THE FUNDAMENTAL PRINCIPLES OF LEGISLATION ON INVESTMENT ACTIVITY IN THE USSR

[Decree of the USSR Supreme Soviet, 10 December 1990. *Vedomosti SND SSSR* (1990), no. 51, item 1110]

The USSR Supreme Soviet decrees:

1. To introduce the Fundamental Principles of Legislation on investment activity in the USSR into effect from 1 January 1991.

2. The union and autonomous republic supreme soviets shall:

bring the legislation of the union and autonomous republics into conformity with the Fundamental Principles of Legislation on Investment Activity in the USSR;

adopt legislative acts on investment activity by taking into account the present Fundamental Principles, national, regional, and other peculiarities but not permitting discriminatory limitations in so doing.

3. The USSR Council of Ministers shall, before 1 July 1991:

submit to the USSR Supreme Soviet proposals concerning the bringing of prevailing legislative acts into conformity with the Fundamental Principles of Legislation on Investment Activity in the USSR;

bring regulations of the Government of the USSR into conformity with the present Fundamental Principles;

ensure the review and repeal by ministries and departments of the USSR of their normative acts, including instructions, which are contrary to the present Fundamental Principles.

4. Until the legislation of the USSR and union republics is brought into conformity with the present Fundamental Principles, prevailing acts of legislation of the USSR and union and autonomous republics shall be applied insofar as they are not contrary to these Fundamental Principles. In so doing, decisions of the Government of the USSR and governments of the union and autonomous republics issued before the introduction into effect of the present Fundamental Principles with regard to questions which according to the Fundamental Principles may be regulated only by legislative acts shall operate until the adoption of the respective legislative acts. The Fundamental Principles of Legislation on Investment Activity in the USSR shall apply to legal relations arising after the introduction of the Fundamental Principles into effect; that is, from 1 January 1991.

With regard to legal relations which arose before 1 January 1991, the Fundamental Principles of Legislation on Investment Activity in the USSR shall apply to those rights and duties which arise after the introduction of the present Fundamental Principles into effect.

Annexes

ON FOREIGN INVESTMENTS IN THE USSR

[Edict of the President of the USSR, 26 October 1990. *Izvestiia*, 26 October 1990, p. 1, cols. 4-6]

With a view to activising the participation of the USSR in world economic links and satisfying more fully on this basis the requirements of the country for products and services by attracting in the form of foreign investments additional material and financial resources, progressive foreign technology, and management experience, I decree:

1. Foreign investors (juridical persons and citizens) may effectuate investments on the territory of the USSR by way of share participation in enterprises organised jointly with Soviet juridical persons and citizens; the acquisition of property, stocks, and other securities; the acquisition autonomously or with the participation of Soviet juridical persons or citizens of the rights to use land and other property rights, including the acquisition of rights in a long-term lease, in accordance with legislation of the USSR and the union and autonomous republics.

Enterprises with foreign investments shall be created in any forms provided for by legislation of the USSR and the union and autonomous republics.

2. Investors (juridical persons and citizens) may create on the territory of the USSR enterprises in which the foreign investments comprise 100% of the property. Such enterprises shall be juridical persons according to Soviet legislation.

3. Foreign investments on the territory of the USSR shall enjoy legal protection and their regime may not be less favourable than the respective regime for the property of Soviet enterprises, organisations, and citizens of the USSR.

4. The profits of foreign investors received in the USSR in Soviet currency may be freely reinvested and used on the territory of the USSR in accordance with legislation of the USSR and union republics, and also transferred abroad in the procedure established by legislation of the USSR.

5. With a view to activising joint entrepreneurial activity with foreign investors in individual areas of the USSR, joint entrepreneurship zones may be created.

The procedure for the effectuation of economic activity of Soviet enterprises and enterprises with foreign investments, as well as granting them privileges, shall be established in each such zone by legislation of the USSR and the union and autonomous republics and by decisions of the respective soviets of people's deputies within the limits of their competence.

Annexes

FUNDAMENTAL PRINCIPLES OF LEGISLATION ON FOREIGN INVESTMENTS IN THE USSR

[Adopted by the USSR Supreme Soviet, 5 July 1991.
Izvestiia, 24 July 1991, p. 4, cols. 1-7]

The present FPForInv shall determine the general principles of effectuating foreign investments on the territory of the USSR directed towards ensuring the effective use in the national economy of the USSR of foreign material and financial resources, modern foreign technology, scientific-technical achievements, and management experience, and shall guarantee the protection of the rights of foreign investors.

Annexes

Section I: General Provisions

Article 1: Legislation on Foreign Investments of USSR and Republics

Relations connected with foreign investments on the territory of the USSR shall be regulated by legislation of the USSR and republics with the exceptions provided for by the present FPForInv and other legislation of the USSR and republics on foreign investments. Relations connected with foreign investments on their territories shall be regulated by legislation of the republics in accordance with the present FPForInv, taking into account the peculiarities of economic activity and investment policy of the republics, except for relations whose regulation has been relegated to the jurisdiction of the USSR, and also relations the duty to regulate which by the USSR arises from international treaties of the USSR.

Article 2: Foreign Investors

There may be foreign investors in the USSR:

(a)   foreign juridical persons;

(b)   foreign citizens, and also stateless persons and citizens of the USSR having a permanent place of residence abroad;

(c)   foreign associations not having the rights of a juridical person;

(d)   foreign States;

(e)   international organisations.

Article 3: Foreign Investments and Forms of Effectuating Them

All types of property and property rights, including the rights to the results of intellectual activity and other rights not relating to [rights in] things, contributed by foreign investors to objects of entrepreneurial activity for the purposes of obtaining a profit or the transfer of knowledge shall be foreign investments.

Foreign investors may effectuate investments on the territory of the USSR by means of:

(a)   share participation in enterprises and organisations jointly with Soviet juridical persons and citizens;

(b)   the creation of enterprises which belong wholly to foreign investors;

(c)   the acquisition of property, including stocks and other securities;

(d)   the acquisition of the rights of use of land and other natural resources, and also other property rights autonomously or with the participation of Soviet juridical persons and citizens;

(e)   the conclusion of contracts with Soviet juridical persons and citizens providing for other forms of effectuating foreign investments.

Article 4: Participation of Foreign Investors in Destatisation and Privatisation of Enterprises

Foreign juridical persons and citizens, foreign associations not having the rights of a juridical person, international organisations, and also stateless persons and citizens of the USSR having a permanent place of residence abroad, may participate in destatisation and privatisation of enterprises in all-union, republic, and municipal ownership on the territory of the USSR.

The said foreign investors may acquire in the established procedure an enterprise (or share) in all-union ownership with the consent of labour collectives in the event that Soviet subjects refuse to acquire such enterprises (or shares) and with the authorisation of the State Property Fund of the USSR.

The conditions of participation of the said investors in destatisation and privatisation of enterprises in republic and municipal ownership shall be determined by legislation of the republics.

Article 5: Legal Regime of Foreign Investments

The legal regime of foreign investments on the territory of the USSR may not be less favourable than the respective regime for property and nonproperty rights, and also of the investment activity, of Soviet enterprises, organisations, and citizens, with the exceptions provided for by legislative acts of the USSR and republics on foreign investments.

Additional tax and other privileges may be established for foreign investments in priority branches of the economy and for individual territories by legislation of the USSR and republics.

Article 6: Types of Activity

Foreign investors and enterprises with foreign investments may effectuate any types of activity unless they have been prohibited by legislative acts of the USSR and republics.

Foreign investors and enterprises with foreign investments may engage in individual types of activity, a list of which shall be determined by legislative acts of the USSR and republics, only on the basis of a special authorisation (or license).

Article 7: Territorial Limitations for Foreign Investments

Territories on which the activity of foreign investors andenterprises with foreign investments are limited or prohibited may be determined by legislative acts of the USSR and republics by proceeding from considerations of ensuring defence and national security.

Article 8: State Foreign Investments Agency

The working out and realisation of all-union policy relating to attracting and using foreign investments, coordination of investment activity, rendering assistance to foreign investors and enterprises with foreign investments in their activities on the territory of the USSR shall be effectuated by a State agency within the jurisdiction of the USSR Cabinet of Ministers, members of which shall be representatives of the republics.

Annexes

Section II: Guarantees of Foreign Investments

Article 9: Guarantees Against Change of Legislation

In the event that subsequent legislation of the USSR and republics worsens the conditions of investing, then the legislation which prevailed at the moment of effectuating the investments shall apply to the foreign investments for ten years.

This provision shall not extend to changes of legislation of the USSR and republics affecting the ensuring of defence, national security, and public order; taxation, credits and finances; environmental protection, and the morality and health of the populace; and also antimonopoly legislation.

Article 10: Guarantees Against Nationalisation and Requisition

Foreign investments in the USSR shall not be subject to nationalisation except for instances when it is effectuated in accordance with legislative acts of the USSR and republics.

Foreign investments shall not be subject to requisition except for instances of natural calamities, wrecks, epidemics, epizootics, and other circumstances of an extraordinary character. Measures relating to requisition shall be adopted by decision of agencies of State power.

Measures relating to nationalisation and requisition must not be of a discriminatory character. In the event such measures are adopted, prompt, adequate, and effective compensation shall be paid to the foreign investor. It shall be paid without unsubstantiated delay, and must correspond to the real value of the investment at the moment the decision concerning nationalisation or measures relating to requisition was adopted. Compensation shall be paid in foreign currency and at the wish of the investor may be transferred abroad.

Disputes concerning the amounts of compensation and the periods and procedure for paying it shall be settled in the USSR in courts in accordance with legislative acts of the USSR and republics, and also in an arbitration court if such has been provided for by agreement of the parties or by an international treaty of the USSR.

Article 11: Guarantees in Event of Termination of Investment Activity

A foreign investor shall, in the event of the termination of investment activity, have the right to compensation for investments due him and revenues received in connection therewith in cash or goods form according to the real value at the moment of terminating investment activity.

Article 12: Guarantees of Transfer of Revenues and Other Amounts in Foreign Currency

The transfer abroad of their revenues and other amounts in foreign currency received on legal grounds in connection with investments shall be guaranteed to foreign investors.

Article 13: Guarantees of Use of Profits in Currency of USSR

The profit of foreign investors received on the territory of the USSR in the currency of the USSR may be reinvested on the territory of the USSR and used in accordance with legislative acts of the USSR and republics. Foreign investors may have accounts in rubles in empowered banks of the USSR.

Foreign investors may use ruble assets in their accounts for the acquisition of foreign currency at the exchange rates formed within the framework of forms authorised by legislation of the USSR for the purchase and sale of foreign currency for rubles.

Annexes

Section III: Creation and Activity of Enterprises with Foreign Investments

Article 14: Enterprises with Foreign Investments

By enterprises with foreign investments is understood enterprises with the participation of foreign investors (or joint enterprises) and enterprises belonging wholly to foreign investors.

Enterprises with foreign investments shall be Soviet juridical persons.

Enterprises with foreign investments shall be created in the form of joint-stock societies, limited responsibility societies, and other economic societies and partnerships, and also in any other forms which are not contrary to legislative acts of the USSR and republics.

A decision concerning the creation of a joint enterprise shall be adopted by its founders autonomously. In the event that the Soviet participant is a State enterprise of an enterprise of a social organisation, the decision concerning the creation of the joint enterprise shall be adopted by its founders with the consent of the owner of the property or agency empowered by it.

A decision concerning the creation of an enterprise belonging wholly to a foreign investor shall be adopted in the procedure determined by legislative acts of the republic on whose territory such enterprise is created.

The peculiarities of creating banks with foreign investments shall be established by legislative acts of the USSR on banks and bank activities.

Article 15: Ecological and Sanitary-Hygienic Expert Examination

When creating an enterprise with foreign investments its founders shall be obliged in the instances and in the procedure provided for by legislation of the USSR and republics to receive the opinion of an expert examination with respect to compliance with sanitary-hygienic and ecological requirements. During the period of activity and at the moment of liquidation, an enterprise with foreign investments shall be obliged to obtain such an opinion.

Article 16: Registration

An enterprise with foreign investments shall be subject to registration in the procedure established by legislative acts of the republics. Requirements for the constitutive and other documents needed to effectuate registration shall be established by legislation of the USSR and republics.

An enterprise with foreign investments shall acquire the rights of a juridical person from the moment of registration. A communication concerning registration shall be published in the press by the agency effectuating the registration.

Data concerning rgistration of enterprises with foreign investments shall be included in republic registers and in the unified State register of the USSR, which shall be kept by the State foreign investments agency.

A refusal of registration may be appealed in the USSR in the courts.

Article 17: Branches and Representations

An enterprise with foreign investments may create branches, representations, and other solitary subdivisions in the USSR and abroad.

On the territory of the USSR branches, representations, and other solitary subdivisions shall not be juridical persons and shall be created while complying with the conditions established by legislation of the USSR and republics for the creation of enterprises.

Article 18: Subsidiary Enterprises

An enterprise with foreign investments may create subsidiary enterprises in the USSR and abroad.

On the territory of the USSR subsidiary enterprises shall be created as juridical persons in accordance with legislation of the USSR and republics.

Article 19: Associations of Enterprises

Enterprises with foreign investments may unite into associations [*assotsiatsii*], concerns, consortiums, and other associations on the conditions and in the procedure provided for by legislative acts of the USSR and republics. Such enterprises may join associations previously created.

Article 20: Making of Contributions by Participants of Joint Enterprise

The periods, amount, and procedure for making and valuing contributions of each participant to the charter fund of a joint enterprise shall be provided for in the constitutive documents. The value of property contributed by the participants of a joint enterprise as a contribution to the charter fund of an enterprise shall be determined by arrangements between the participants of the joint enterprise.

In the absence upon the expiry of a year after registration of documentary confirmation of the fact of each participant paying in 50% of the contributions specified in the constitutive documents to the charter fund, the agency which has registered the said joint enterprise shall deem it to be insolvent and shall exclude it from the register of joint enterprises. Information concerning exclusion from the register shall be published in the press.

Article 21: Reserve Fund

At enterprises with foreign investments a reserve fund shall be created in an amount of up to 25% of the charter fund. The formation of the reserve fund shall be effectuated by means of annual deductions both in currency of the USSR and in foreign currency. The amount of annual deductions to the reserve fund and the types of currency shall be determined by the enterprise autonomously.

Article 22: Realisation of Product and Delivery on Territory of USSR

An enterprise with foreign investments shall have the right on a contractual basis to establish prices for the produce (or work, service) produced by it, determine the procedure for realising it on the internal market of the USSR, and select suppliers of the produce (or work, services) from this market.

Article 23: Accounts in Foreign Currency on Territory of USSR

The use of foreign currency, and also payments documents in foreign currency, when effectuating accounts on the territory of the USSR by enterprises with foreign investments shall be permitted in the procedure established by legislation of the USSR on currency regulation.

Article 24: Export and Import of Product

Enterprises with foreign investments in whose charter fund foreign investments comprise 15% or more shall have the right to export without licenses a product (or work, service) of their own production. An enterprise with foreign investments shall have the right without licenses to effectuate the import of the product (or work, service) for its own economic activity.

The procedure for relegating a product (or work, service) to a product of the own production of enterprises with foreign investments shall be established by legislation of the USSR.

Article 25: Currency Receipts

The currency receipts of an enterprise with foreign investments shall remain at his disposition on condition of complying with legislation of the USSR on currency regulation.

Article 26: Customs Levy

Property imported into the USSR as the contribution of a foreign investor to the charter fund of a joint enterprise or in order to create an enterprise belonging wholly to a foreign investor shall be exempt from payment of customs duty and shall not be levied with tax on import.

Property imported into the USSR by foreign workers of an enterprise with foreign investments for their own needs shall be exempt from the payment of customs duty.

Article 27: Insurance

The insurance of property and risks of an enterprise with foreign investments shall be effectuated at its discretion, unless compulsory insurance has been provided for by legislation of the USSR and republics.

Article 28: Taxation

Enterprises with foreign investments, and also foreign investors, shall pay the taxes established by legislative acts of the USSR and republics.

Article 29: Verification of Activity of Enterprises with Foreign Investments

Tax and other agencies to whom the verification of individual aspects of the activity of enterprises with foreign investments has been entrusted may effectuate such verifications as the need arises and strictly within the limits of their competence. Enterprises shall submit to such agencies respective reports and documentation concerning their activities. Tax and other agencies shall be obliged to ensure the keeping of commercial secrecy.

Verification for the purposes of taxation of financial and commercial activity of such enterprises shall be effectuated by auditor organisations empowered in accordance with legislation of the USSR and republics for carrying on such activity.

Article 30: Records and Reports

An enterprise with foreign investments shall effectuate operational and bookkeeping records and keep statistical reports in accordance with the rules prevailing in the USSR.

Article 31: Securing Obligations

The property of an enterprise with foreign investments may be used by it in accordance with legislation of the USSR and republics as security for all types of its obligations, including the attraction of borrowed assets. Its property rights to buildings, installations, equipment, and other property rights, including the right to use land and other natural resources, also may be security.

Article 32: Rights to Results of Intellectual Activity and Other Rights Not Relating to [Rights to] Thing

The protection of rights, provided as foreign investments, to the results of intellectual activity, and also other rights not relating to [the rights to] a thing (know-how, commercial secret, and others) shall be ensured by legislative acts of the USSR and republics.

The use of the results of intellectual activity received at enterprises with foreign investments shall be effectuated in accordance with legislative acts of the USSR and republics.

Article 33: Labour Relations

Production and labour relations, including questions of hiring and dismissal, the regime of labour and leisure, payment of labour, guarantees and compensation at enterprises with foreign investments shall be regulated by the collective contract (or agreement) and individual labour contracts.

The conditions of collective and individual labour contracts may not worsen the position of workers of that enterprise in comparison with the conditions provided for by legislative acts of the USSR and republics.

Questions of the payment of labour, granting of leaves, and the pension security of foreign workers of an enterprise with foreign investments must be decided in individual labour contracts with each of them. The earnings received by such workers in foreign currency may be transferred by them abroad.

Article 34: Social Insurance and Security

Social insurance of workers of an enterprise with foreign investments and the social security thereof (except for pension security of foreign workers) shall be regulated by the norms of Soviet legislation.

An enterprise with foreign investments shall transfer payments for pension security of foreign workers to the respective funds of the countries of their permanent place of residence in the currency of those countries.

An enterprise shall make deductions for State social insurance of Soviet and foreign workers and deductions for the pension security of Soviet workers according to the rates established for Soviet enterprises and organisations.

Article 35: Liquidation

An enterprise with foreign investments may be liquidated in the procedure and instances provided for by legislative acts of the USSR and republics.

The accumulated assets of an enterprise with foreign investments shall, when it is liquidated, be subject to taxation at their real value.

Annexes

Section IV: Acquisition of Securities by Foreign Investors

Article 36: Acquisition of State Securities

The acquisition by foreign investors of State securities shall be effectuated in the procedure determined by the empowered State agency.

Article 37: Acquisition of Securities of Soviet Juridical Persons

Foreign investors shall have the right to acquire stocks and other securities of Soviet juridical persons for foreign currency and currency of the USSR in the procedure and on the conditions determined by legislation of the USSR and republics.

Annexes

Section V: Acquisition by Foreign Investors of Rights to Use Land and Other Property Rights

Article 38: Right to Use Land

Land, including the lease thereof, may be granted for use to foreign investors and enterprises with foreign investments in accordance with legislation of the USSR and republics on land.

In the event of the transfer of ownership to a structure or installation, the right to use the land plot shall pass together with those objects in the procedure and on the conditions established by legislation of the republics.

Article 39: Right to Use Resources of Economic Zone of USSR and Continental Shelf of USSR

The right to explore, work, and exploit the natural resources of the economic zone of the USSR and the continental shelf of the USSR may be granted to foreign investors and enterprises with foreign investments in accordance with legislation of the USSR and republics on the economic zone of the USSR and continental shelf of the USSR.

Article 40: Lease

The lease of property to foreign investors and enterprises with foreign investments shall be effectuated by the lessor on the basis of contracts and in accordance with legislative acts of the USSR and republics on lease and lease relations.

Article 41: Concession Contracts

The granting to foreign investors of concessions for the exploration, working, and exploitation of renewable and nonrenewable natural resources and for conducting other economic activity shall be effectuated on the basis of concession contracts concluded by foreign investors with empowered agencies of the USSR and republics in the procedure determined by legislative acts of the USSR and republics.

The conditions of effectuating activity of foreign investors shall be determined in the concession contract. Conditions differing from provisions established by legislative acts of the USSR and republics may be contained therein within the limits of the competence respectively of the USSR and republics.

The unilateral change of the conditions of a concession contract shall not be permitted, unless stipulated otherwise in the contract.

Annexes

Section VI: Foreign Investments in Free Economic Zones

Article 42: Activity of Foreign Investors and Enterprises With Foreign Investments in Free Economic Zones

A territory in which a special regime of economic activity of foreign investors and enterprises with foreign investments is established, and also of Soviet enterprises and citizens, shall be a free economic zone in the USSR.

The procedure for the effectuation of economic activity of foreign investors and enterprises with foreign investments and the conditions of privileged export-import, tax, customs, currency, banking, and other types of regulation in each such zone shall be established by legislation of the USSR and republics and by decisions of the respective soviets of people's deputies within the limits of their competence.

A decision concerning the creation of each zone shall be adopted in the procedure established by legislative acts of the republics.

Annexes

Section VII: Concluding Provisions

Article 43: Consideration of Disputes

Disputes between foreign investors and the State shall be subject to consideration in the USSR in courts unless provided otherwise by international treaties of the USSR.

Disputes of foreign investors and of enterprises with foreign investments with Soviet State agencies acting as parties in relations regulated by civil legislation, enterprises, social organisations, and other Soviet juridical persons, a dispute between the participants of an enterprise with foreign investments, and also disputes between the participants of an enterprise with foreign investments and the enterprise itself shall be subject to consideration in the USSR in courts or, by arrangement of the parties, by way of arbitration, including abroad, and in the instances provided for by legislative acts of the USSR and republics, in arbitrazh courts, economic courts, and others.

Article 44: International Treaties

If other rules have been established by international treaties than those which are contained in legislation of the USSR and republics on foreign investments, the rules of the international treaty shall be applied.

ON THE INTRODUCTION INTO EFFECT OF THE FUNDAMENTAL PRINCIPLES OF LEGISLATION ON FOREIGN INVESTMENTS IN THE USSR

[Decree of the USSR Supreme Soviet, 5 July 1991.
Izvestiia, 24 July 1991, p. 4, cols. 4-7]

The USSR Supreme Soviet decrees:

1. To introduce the Fundamental Principles of Legislation on Foreign Investments in the USSR into effect from the moment of their publication.

2. The USSR Cabinet of Ministers shall before 1 October 1991:

determine with the participation of the governments of the republics and submit to the USSR Supreme Soviet for confirmation a list of priority branches of the economy, including science, education, public health, and culture, and also territories in which it is advisable to grant additional tax and other privileges to foreign investors;

prepare with the participation of the governments of the republics and confirm a Statute on the State Foreign Investments Agency;

work out with the participation of the governments of the republics and confirm the procedure for relegation products, (or work, services) to products of own production of enterprises with foreign investments;

determine the State agency for the issuance of State securities and authorise it to work out the procedure and conditions for acquiring such securities by foreign investors;

submit to the USSR Supreme Soviet proposals concerning the bringing of legislative acts of the USSR into conformity with the Fundamental Principles of Legislation on Foreign Investments in the USSR;

bring into conformity with the said FPForInv decisions of the Government of the USSR;

ensure the review and repeal by ministries, State committees, and departments of the USSR of their normative acts, including instructions, which are contrary to the said FPForInv.

3. The USSR Cabinet of Ministers shall, when deciding practical questions connected with foreign investments, promote the use above all of the work force and material resources of the USSR and republics.

4. The State Bank of the USSR shall work out and introduce into effect the regime for ruble accounts for foreign investors.

5.   To establish that:

the procedure for determining the rate of tax on profit provided for by Article 5(3) of the Law of the USSR "On Taxes from Enterprises, Associations, and Organisations" shall not extend to enterprises with foreign investments;

enterprises belonging wholly to foreign investors shall be levied with taxes on the conditions and in the procedure established for joint enterprises, the share of foreign participation in the charter fund of which exceeds 30%.

6.   To recommend to the republic supreme soviets to adopt legislative acts on foreign investments and to bring legislation of the republics into conformity with the said FPForInv.